Making the Most of Middle School

A Field Guide for Parents and Others

Making the Most of Middle School

A Field Guide for Parents and Others

Anthony W. Jackson and
P. Gayle Andrews
with
Holly Holland and
Priscilla Pardini

Teachers College, Columbia University
New York and London

Published by Teachers College Press, 1234 Amsterdam Avenue, New York, NY 10027

Library of Congress Cataloging-in-Publication Data

Making the most of middle school : A field guide for parents and others / Anthony W. Jackson ... [et al.].
   p. cm.
  Includes bibliographical references and index
  ISBN 0-8077-4476-X (pbk. : alk. paper)
    1. Middle school education—United States. 2. Teenagers—Education—United States. 3. School improvement programs—United States. I. Jackson, Anthony (Anthony Wells)
  LB1623.5.M55 2004
  373.236—dc22   2003068736

ISBN 0-8077-4476-X (paper)

Printed on acid-free paper
Manufactured in the United States of America

11 10 09 08 07 06 05 04   8   7   6   5   4   3   2   1

Contents

Introduction

He sleeps with stuffed animals but stands up to racist adults. He eloquently debates laws during a mock legislature at the state capitol but forgets to change his underwear for a week. He knows more about Greek mythology than Homer but can't recall what he is supposed to do for homework tonight.

Meet my son, the middle school student. I love him. He drives me crazy. I think he's one of the most miraculous creatures on earth. His 8th grade classmates voted him "Most Unpredictable." Capricious, thy name is Dylan!

HOLLY WROTE THOSE LINES IN THE SPRING OF 2002. As a parent and the former editor of *Middle Ground* magazine, a professional journal that National Middle School Association publishes for educators, she knows what it's like to have a teenager in transition. The rest of us are parents, too, although our children are just entering the middle school years. But we bring our experience to bear. Tony, for example, is the primary author of a landmark report on early adolescent education, *Turning Points: Preparing American Youth for the 21st Century* and co-author with Gayle of the equally influential follow-up study, *Turning Points 2000: Educating Adolescents in the 21st Century*. Gayle is an assistant professor of middle-level education at the University of Georgia. And Priscilla is a former middle-grades teacher who has spent the past 15 years working as a writer specializing in education.

Throughout our work, we have analyzed the lessons of research and the wisdom of practical experience for insights into how to help our own children succeed in school. One thing we have learned is that, no matter how much we might know about a subject professionally, we will never stop learning as parents.

In the past decade, professional educators have discovered more about middle-grades children than at any other point in history. We know how they learn, how they mature, and how they feel. We know why they need to make healthy choices to ensure their optimum physical and mental development, and we understand why they need strong relationships with adults who can help them navigate the slippery slopes of adolescence. We appreciate how they soar when talented teachers tickle their imaginations and expand their intellectual capacity. Sadly, we also have seen their spark of creativity grow cold in schools that are as large and anonymous as department stores. The more we use this knowledge to help our children grow up well, the more all of us will benefit.

"I think I'm on a good path because my mom is always guiding me," an 8th grader from Texas told us during an interview for this book. "My mom always tells me, 'Don't be scared to tell me things. I'm here to help you.'"

Unfortunately, research reveals that many parents disengage from their children's schools during the middle years. Even parents who were actively involved with their children's elementary school education find themselves confused about their changing roles as their offspring enter the middle grades. Most parents realize that the techniques that worked so well when their children were younger—such as volunteering in the classroom, chaperoning class trips, or supervising their children's homework—may no longer be appreciated, or appropriate. But they don't know what else to try. Add to that an adolescent's natural desire for greater freedom from parental authority and many schools' lack of interest in working with parents, and it's no wonder that some parents drop out of the middle school picture altogether. Often, their children disengage from school too.

For many young people, in large part because of the caring and committed people who nurture them in middle school, their paths lead to unlimited potential. But for some adolescents, the unfortunate mismatch between their intellectual, social, and emotional needs and the services offered by their middle schools may put them on a path toward a greatly diminished future.

Forming partnerships to improve schools is new territory for families and educators in the middle grades. Both groups need to understand their rights and responsibilities and the reasons why they must work together. With politicians and the public demanding higher academic standards and greater achievement than ever before, schools can no longer afford to give families the cold shoulder. As Anne T. Henderson and Nancy Berla wrote in their 1994 report of 66 studies linking parent involvement to children's learning: "The evidence is now beyond dispute. When schools work together with families to support learning, children tend to succeed not just in school, but throughout life."

Reading this book will help you reconnect with the children you parent and teach. It includes authentic stories about some of the 9.2 million middle-level students in the United States, engaging examples from some of their best teachers, and practical advice about how parents and teachers can work together for the betterment of all children.

Among the valuable research reflected in this book are the most important features of the groundbreaking report, *Turning Points*, published in 1989, and its follow-up, *Turning Points 2000*, which discussed the progress made in middle-level education since that time. Both the report and the book were written primarily for middle-schools teachers and administrators. We wrote this book to help you—parents, teachers, and school and community leaders—to understand how to educate children in the middle and to advocate for schools that use those practices recommended by the research.

Holly reports that her own middle-schooler has matured into a responsible high school sophomore who only occasionally forgets his homework. Like all of us, Holly knows that adolescents are interesting, passionate, and capable people who become temporarily inconsistent between the ages of 10 and 14.

1

Children in the Middle

"It takes work, but I can do it," said Terry[1], referring to the challenging assignments he receives from some of his teachers at a large, diverse public middle school in Kentucky. About 40% of the students are African American like Terry, and about 10% are immigrants from around the world.

An 8th grader, Terry enjoys problem solving and thinking about new ideas, "things that I've never heard of." His favorite subject is math and his worst is English.

"In language arts, we always have to write and I can't come up with ideas that quickly," he said. Although he doesn't enjoy writing, he praised his 7th grade language arts teacher for helping him brainstorm topics and for insisting that he could improve his skills. Likewise, his 7th grade math teacher made learning fun by giving different numbers fake names, "and then when she told us the [mathematical] function, it was easy to learn."

When he was in the 3rd grade, Terry tested into the school system's advanced program, giving him access to accelerated classes. He said he usually starts his homework as soon as he gets home from school, a habit his grandmother reinforces. In this way, she lets him know that she cares about his education.

Terry wants to be a computer technician when he grows up. He collects sports trading cards and spends his free time playing on the computer and reading. He enjoys mysteries the most.

An engaging and big-hearted boy who tries to keep his classmates feeling upbeat, Terry usually looks forward to going to school. He plays a per-

---

[1] The children's names have been changed to protect their privacy.

cussion instrument in the school band and earned regional honors for his musical skills. In addition, he competes on the school's academic team.

If he were in charge of designing a middle school, Terry said he would make sure that no class had more than 15 students—instead of the 34 he is accustomed to—and that students could choose at least two of their six subjects. He would want the assignments to be "a little harder," the teachers "a little nicer," and the student population to exclude "people that don't care about school."

As a 6th grader, Jason already is planning to attend "a good college." He knows that colleges expect students to have high grades, so he tries to earn them. He knows that colleges appreciate a record of community service, so he continues working toward his Eagle Scout rank. He knows that graduating from a top-notch high school will improve his chances of getting into a prestigious university, so he plans to graduate from the private Florida academy he has attended since kindergarten.

But for all his foresight and advantages, Jason can't remember ever being happy in the classroom. "I've never actually liked school," he said. "The thing is, no kid really likes school. The only reason anyone likes school is they like to see their friends."

Asked to describe an interesting course or an engaging teacher, Jason can't think of a single example. He can recall plenty of unsatisfactory instruction, however, including the way his authoritarian science teacher treats students with disdain. "She doesn't give you much choice," he said. "She's like, 'If you don't do this my way, you get grades off.'"

Math is his best class. "In math, I want to someday skip a grade. I don't want to be considered one of the really dumb kids. Then you get picked on a lot." But Jason also doesn't want to be one of the kids who are considered "geeks. I like where I am right now, in the middle."

It bothers him somewhat that his school is not diverse—ethnically, racially, or economically. He is a white male surrounded by other white faces, with a small number of students from Colombia and India. "Now there are two black students in my grade," he said. "Last year there were none."

An articulate and self-motivated boy who takes pride in his ability to juggle many responsibilities, Jason wishes he were more athletic so he would "never get picked on." He's focusing on the middle school soccer team, where he hopes to earn a position as a midfielder. "Probably not," though, he says without bitterness. "I'm not that good. A lot of kids at school are better than me."

Jason is an avid reader—fantasy novels such as *The Chronicles of Narnia* are his favorites. He also enjoys playing video games and a card game called *Magic: The Gathering*, in which players build decks of their best cards in hopes of beating their opponents through strategy.

Jason would like to pursue a career as a weapons designer, focusing on smart machines that could disable tanks, for example, but not hurt people. He's also considering becoming an "Apache pilot" so he could navigate the U.S. Army's large helicopters.

With her broad smile, positive attitude, and thick bangs framing a small, round face, Sylvia presents the picture of a happy, carefree adolescent. She is a 12-year-old Texas 7th grader who attends a public middle school with about 800 students, most of them Latino.

Appearances aside, Sylvia copes with a great deal of stress. Her father died recently and she and her mother and sister had to move in with relatives—11 family members living in one small house.

Sylvia bears her hardships with impressive maturity, counseling peers who are sexually active to respect themselves more, urging her older sister to stay in school, scolding her grandmother when she eats foods that are bad for her health. It helps that Sylvia belongs to several school-sponsored groups, which keep her focused on academics and community service. One of these groups, which meets weekly after school, started out as a place for girls to gain confidence and self-esteem but later evolved into a reading club. Another school group has raised her awareness of the opportunities teenagers have to make a difference in the world. In that role, Sylvia enjoyed a volunteer stint at a local homeless shelter, where she got to serve food and play with the children.

"It was so exciting because you get to meet somebody from the opposite life and know that you did something to help," she said.

At school, Sylvia earns average grades. Her favorite subjects are math and science, the latter because "you get to do so many experiments." History is Sylvia's least favorite subject because she said her teacher provides little direction with assignments, screams at students in class, and passes out worksheets instead of developing creative and interesting lessons.

"She just puts stuff on the board and tells you to copy it," Sylvia said.

Sylvia wants to be a pediatrician when she grows up. Her interest in medicine stems from a school field trip to a local science museum, where she saw models of the human organs. She was particularly impressed by an exhibit that demonstrated the damage cigarette smoking does to a person's lungs. "Everybody thought it was neat," she said.

Sylvia enjoys reading books, but that wasn't always true. She credits her 6th grade reading teacher with helping her understand *how* to read well, first by requiring students to read at least 20 minutes each night, then by showing them specific strategies for understanding difficult passages, such as scanning a paragraph and mentally reflecting on its meaning before advancing. Sylvia became so engrossed in reading the *Harry Potter* series "that I didn't want to eat. I'd be walking through Wal-Mart and reading and I'd bump into things" because she was paying attention to the story instead of following her mother through the store.

❖   ❖   ❖

"YOU'RE NOT SURE IF YOU'RE AN ADULT OR A KID"

THESE ARE THE FACES OF CHILDREN IN THE MIDDLE, those fast-growing, hard-charging, ever-changing young adolescents who can make their parents and teachers proud, peeved, and perplexed from one minute to the next. On the road from childhood to adulthood, they can be erratic drivers, changing lanes and speeds to keep up with the traffic, taking detours to check out new scenery, hesitating, accelerating, and occasionally running out of gas.

Along with the spurts and pangs of adolescence, they also bring energy, talent, and inspiration to their families, schools, and communities. Some of them lobby members of Congress about child labor practices around the world, while others speak to their local school boards about alternative solutions for budget deficits. Some of them produce radio shows, patent inventions, monitor pollution, and design their own middle schools. They are published authors, accomplished musicians, and Web designers. Together they raise millions of dollars for charity each year.

One group of 6th graders decided to teach citizenship skills to their peers and neighbors by involving them in a plan to improve a local road. In addition to conducting traffic surveys and analyzing problems, they worked with a highway engineer, a construction company, local conservationists, and political leaders to design and build a new pedestrian path and bridge.

"Service is a habit, and like most habits, it is most effectively developed at an early age," concluded the Corporation for National and Community Service in its 2002 report, *Students in Service to America.*

During the all-important middle years, the time between the ages of 10 and 14, adolescents try out new roles and develop habits that can last for a day, for a week, or for a lifetime. As the previous profiles suggest, the middle years represent a fascinating period of physical, intellectual, and social changes. During puberty, growth is more rapid than at any other developmental stage except infancy. But this intense expansion can be uneven, which is why one 13-year-old might need to borrow his father's shaving supplies and another might need a stepstool to reach the water fountain.

The onset of body hair, menstruation, acne, voice changes, and braces—all of these physical rites of passage tend to occur in the middle grades, evincing every emotion from embarrassment to excitement, usually depending on the reactions of others. Young adolescents are supremely self-conscious and are hungry for attention and nourishment—physical, intellectual, and spiritual. They often prefer active, loud, and energetic activities and need regular opportunities for exercise and stimulation. Some adolescents actually feel growing pains as their bones lengthen, their muscles stretch, and their weight shifts. No wonder they hate sitting at hard desks all day in school!

All of these changes can make middle-grades students feel tired, confused, and irritable, so it's more important than ever that they get adequate sleep and have periods of quiet and reflection throughout the day.

Hardest Part About Being a Teenager	Girls	Boys
Peer Pressure	37%	21%
Expectations/Responsibilities	20%	24%
Avoiding Drugs/Sex/Alcohol/Criminal Activities	18%	17%
Other	11%	11%
Academics	5%	15%
Nothing	2%	10%
Puberty/Sexual Feelings	6%	3%

Note: Due to rounding, totals do not equal 100%.

With such swift fluctuations in their physical and hormonal development, young adolescents can experience emotional peaks and valleys and are particularly vulnerable to hurt and humiliation. They are extremely sensitive to ridicule and harbor strong self-doubts.

As part of our research for this book, we surveyed 2,369 middle-grades students in eight U.S. states, collecting a national sampling[2] of opinions about a wide range of topics. The students live in urban, suburban, and rural communities, attend public and private schools of various sizes and configurations, and celebrate distinctive family and cultural traditions. No matter their background or interests, all of the students have strong opinions.

What's the hardest part about being a teenager today, we asked in one of the survey questions? Peer pressure was the number one response, with 30% of students saying they have a tough time standing up to other adolescents and another 5% specifically mentioning problems with the "opposite sex."

"The girls and guys," an 8th grader fretted. "They are complicating."

"Trying to find your true love," was how another 8th grader described his greatest difficulty.

---

[2] For a detailed look at the survey questions and methodology, please see the Appendix.

For a 7th grade girl, "The hardest part about being a teenager today is trying to be normal."

Specific challenges included:

> "Fitting in and knowing who your real friends are."
>
> "Being teased because you're different and seeing it happen to others."
>
> "Feeling that you are all alone and sad and don't fit in anywhere."
>
> "You never know if you are popular enough for a crowd."
>
> "Escaping the consistent display of pathetic manlihood."
>
> "Contrary to what most people think, it's not refusing drugs. It's more of a self-acceptance issue than anything else."

Students also complained about "parents!," "mean teachers!," and "going through body changes." In addition, large numbers worry about the increasing responsibilities at home and at school.

> "You're not sure if you're an adult or a kid," said a 13-year-old.
>
> "People expect so much, or too little of you," one 8th grader said.
>
> "Fitting everything into your schedule and getting up so early," a 6th grader complained.
>
> "Everybody wants you to be something you aren't," said a 7th grader.
>
> "I don't think people understand me as much as I would like," another 7th grader added.
>
> "When you were little all you did was eat, drink, sleep," an 8th grader reflected. "Now it's work, work, work, and work."

In our survey, we also asked students what they like about themselves and what they would change if they could. Gender differences surfaced, with more than one-fourth of middle school girls citing their looks and personality as pleasing attributes, while boys most often mentioned their athleticism and intelligence. Specific responses to the question of what they like about themselves included:

What I Like About Myself

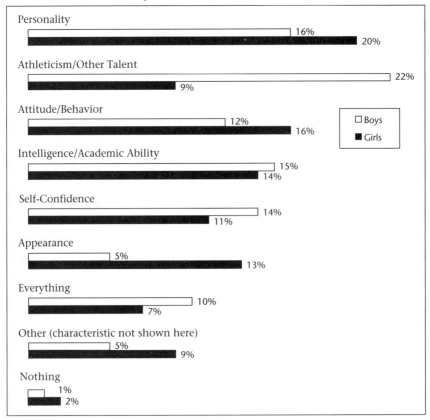

"How smart and unique I am."

"My positive attitude and my friendly nature and my sense of humor."

"That I can trust my judgment most times."

"That I like to volunteer."

"I like that I have lots of really good friends and they all like me."

"I am a hard worker with a good personality."

"That I am not afraid to express myself."

"I like the fact that I am generous and friendly."

What I'd Change About Myself

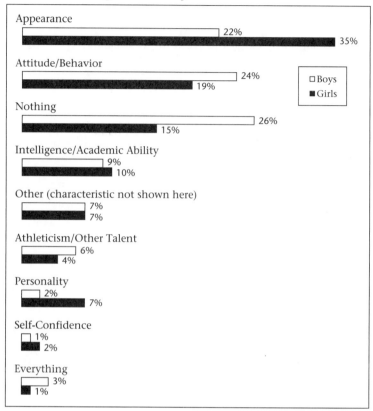

"I have a *great* imagination."

"I love everything except my forehead."

"I'm so darn adorable, you can't help but love me."

In response to the question about what they don't like about themselves, they listed the usual disappointments: They'd like to be smarter, better looking, more athletic, less forgetful, and, depending on what stage of development they happened to be in, to lose or to gain weight. Again, gender differences were pronounced, with 35% of girls lamenting their appearance while the most frequent response from boys was the desire to change "nothing."

Some comments reflect the singularly self-conscious aura that seems to surround students in the middle.

> "I wish I could change my ability to procrastinate," a 13-year-old girl said.
>
> "The fact that I am hyper," another added. "I want to be mysterious!"
>
> An 8th grade boy desired "the will to work harder."
>
> "I wish I made friends easier and was not so loud," said a 7th grade boy.
>
> An 8th grader said she wished she "could change the fact that I am so empathetic that it brings me down."

Acute awareness of the other gender factors into many of their conversations.

> One 11-year-old girl wished she "could be better in sports and make boys like me."
>
> A 6th grade boy said he'd like to be "funnier and a better girl magnet."
>
> "I haven't found anything really hard except boys," an 8th grader told us.

Other desires were more physically explicit.

> "I wish my ears weren't so big," a 12-year-old boy said.
>
> "One thing I would change is the straightness of my foot so I don't walk sideways without knowing it," a boy said.
>
> "My nose—it's *way* too big!" a 7th grade girl told us. "And my nails, I bite them."

Some comments brought up the painful realities of racism and other hostile encounters in the lives of young adolescents.

> "I wish that I can go to stores and people won't stalk me because of my color," a 14-year-old boy told us.
>
> A 6th grader said he would change "my behavior and my race."

> An 11-year-old boy said he wished he would "not get called a geek, loser, mental race, etc."
>
> A 13-year-old boy wanted to "understand why this school's inhabitants loathe me so."

And one 12-year-old girl summed up the angst that anchors so many adolescent emotions. What's one thing you wish you could change about yourself, we asked?

"Everything," she lamented.

Young adolescents want desperately to belong and feel included, which is why they often band together and seek affiliation with groups. Peer influence is strong. One middle school teacher, chuckling at how adolescents rarely separate from the group during social functions, coined the term "amoeba dancing" to refer to their propensity for moving and changing shape en masse.

LEVELING THE PLAYING FIELD

In the process of creating their own identities and finding a place to belong, some students come face to face with unfairness during the middle grades. Poverty plays a significant part. One out of every six American children (16.7%) was poor in 2000, according to figures compiled by the Children's Defense Fund, and the figures were highest for black children (30.6%) and Hispanic children (28%). Contrary to popular belief, more poor children live in suburban and rural areas than in urban centers. Wherever they live, however, poor children have a greater risk of scoring lower on standardized tests, being held back a grade, and failing to finish high school, with the deficits increasing the longer a child remains in poverty.

Poor children have less access to the resources they need to develop well and succeed in school, including learning from quality teachers. Research shows that the adults in charge of 53% of the classes in high-poverty middle schools lacked a college major in the subjects they teach. Schools with high concentrations of poor children also tend to have greater numbers of uncertified teachers and limited access to technology and other materials that can assist in their education. When these deprivations become pervasive, children can get caught in a cycle of failure that stunts their initiative.

Dismissing such inequities as the unfortunate circumstances of other people's children or alternatively viewing the problem as too big to probe won't help. All adolescents need a steady diet of caring, consistency, and challenge in school. Children who get less than others usually don't become skilled employees or contribute to the growth of competitive companies and tax-supported societies. School is one of the few places where children can level the uneven circumstances of their birth, which is why parents must insist that all students—both their own and other people's children—have access to rigorous classes and knowledgeable educators who are committed to their growth.

In its 2001 survey of 40,000 middle and high school students, the Minority Student Achievement Network found that African American and Latino students care as much about school success as do white and Asian American students. Indeed, among males, African Americans were the most likely to report that their friends think it is "very important" to "study hard and get good grades." The network, a coalition of 15 suburban school districts in eight states, found a few differences among ethnic groups. Much higher percentages of African American and Latino students reported having difficulty understanding the teacher's lesson. And those groups were more likely to say they respond best to "teacher encouragement" than "teacher demands." In other words, black and Latino students are more likely than others to work harder in school when their teachers encourage them instead of demand their compliance.

"Kids come to us with different degrees of confidence, motivation, resilience, and engagement," Allan Alson, the founder of the network and the superintendent of the Evanston (Illinois) Township High School District 202, told the newspaper *Education Week*. "Training must sensitize adults to these, not to stereotype kids, but to pick up on the ways kids present themselves and be responsive to that." Educators should do so "not [by] deviating from the curriculum or diminishing standards, but [by] building relationships with kids around the work they do in class. We as educators have to demonstrate to kids we will not give up on them."

For many students, middle school is the time when they become keenly aware of differences—racial, ethnic, religious, economic, and social. Legacies of prejudice and intolerance can exacerbate feelings of inadequacy typically associated with being a minority. Parents and educators strengthen adolescents' self-esteem when they deepen their understanding of our increasingly multicultural society and demonstrate respect for people from all backgrounds.

Studying a variety of cultural traditions can help children develop an appreciation of others and embrace the contributions of their ancestors. However, such study should not be limited to "heroes and holidays," the occasional celebrations that relegate many ethnic groups to the margins of the main curriculum. Instead, middle schools should consistently include resources and perspectives from a wide range of ethnic traditions in all fields.

Along with the normal stresses of everyday life, today's young adolescents also must cope with the complications of divorce and blended families, economic insecurity, and international terrorism. The conflicts that concern them range from global crises to the heartaches and hassles visible from their own backyards.

One student in our survey told us she feared seeing her abusive father again, while other students said they rarely have contact with one or the other parent because of marital separation.

An 8th grader from Maine told us that in her family "it seems like nobody talks to each other."

An Idaho 8th grader was sad about "having to be away from my mom and dad. Because my mom has an illness, and my dad is in Chicago."

Providing evidence of the broad developmental stages they move through during adolescence, many students revealed that they are still afraid of the dark, of being home alone, and of finding monsters in the closet. Other students fear monsters of the modern age, such as "dying from a nuclear war" or "Bin Laden coming into my bedroom and taking me away." Some students fear "catching on fire," "not having any friends," "clowns, gangs, and chickens," "not succeeding," and "the unlived life."

For an increasing number of middle-grades students, such fears are not distant concerns but nightmares from their life experiences.

In many American communities, for example, political refugees who are victims of international conflicts come to classrooms without the emotional, cultural, and language support that most of their peers take for granted. As psychologist Mary Pipher writes in her book *The Middle of Everywhere,* the people who migrate to our shores often have escaped tragedies of almost mythic proportions. They're children whose grandparents carried them "across raging rivers," or whose families "walked barefoot in the snow," trudged across mountain passes, and escaped murderous barbarians. "I've heard children tell of bombs that they thought were fireworks until they saw bodies explode."

Middle schools must make a safe haven for all of these students, ensuring that each child has an adult advocate who provides a beacon in the fog. Adolescence creates many opportunities for students to forge strong identities, to learn new social roles, and to develop a personal code of ethics to guide their behavior—*if* they have relationships with caring and committed adults who can advise them as they grow.

THE FACE OF THE FUTURE

It's important to remember that while adolescence can be a period of stress and uncertainty for many youths, most of them adjust well to the physical, social, and intellectual changes and emerge as healthy and happy teenagers. Parents play a critical role in shaping their success. As their children's first teachers and lifelong guardians, parents are most effective when they know their children's peers and teachers and work with them to steer the children in the right direction. Together, the key people in an adolescent's life can collectively weave what Search Institute fellow Peter Scales calls a positive "web of influence."

In a 1998 survey of young teens, KidsPeace, The National Center for Kids Overcoming Crisis, found that most 13-year-olds would turn to their parents first in a crisis, followed closely by their friends, then by their teachers and principals. By age 15, however, adolescents begin consulting their friends about as often as they seek advice from their parents.

"Today, early-teens want to trust their parents more than their friends, but they feel they cannot," reported KidsPeace, adding that:

> [About] three out of 10 early-teens [32%] tell us they feel uncomfortable raising a difficult topic with their parents. Only two of eleven [18%] said they would feel totally comfortable raising a topic that was very important to them. Age and gender play a key role in determining to whom a teen talks about a problem. Girls are more likely to talk to friends, and boys are more likely to seek the counsel of parents first.

Even among homeless and runaway youth, the connection to parents is critical.

"We are finding that adolescents living away from their homes who still maintain ties to parents have a better chance of eventually returning home," reports UCLA researcher Norweeta Milburn. "As those ties wither, youth are more likely never to return home, and are far more prone to become involved in high risk and criminal behaviors."

Communicating well with young adolescents involves much more than setting rules and demanding compliance. Communication builds from strong connections, nurtured throughout childhood. Middle-grades students need advice about a multitude of decisions from eating a healthy diet and managing their time wisely to negotiating their neighborhoods safely and choosing challenging courses in school. Yet, precisely at the point when adolescents are trying to decide whether to turn to their parents or their peers, family conversations often cease.

According to the University of Michigan's 1997 survey of a nationally representative sample of children ages 12 and under, young adolescents spent the least amount of time talking with their families, an average of 28 minutes a week, or 4 minutes a day, representing a 100% decline since 1981. Today's children actually spend more total time with their parents than children did two decades ago, but the conversations don't go very deep.

One 11-year-old girl wrote in a survey collected for this book that the worst part about her family is that "Nobody pays attention to me most of the time."

Middle-grades students want and need greater freedom than younger children, but they still require close monitoring and supervision. As Hayes Mizell, former director of the Program for Student Achievement at the Edna McConnell Clark Foundation, reflected during a 2002 public lecture in Nyack, New York:

> Children who were once affectionate, trusting, and respectful of adult authority may suddenly become withdrawn, questioning, and critical. Parents are perpetually off-balance as one day their children are joyful and full of life and the next day they act as though life is not worth living. Just when parents believe they have figured out the "rules" of early adolescent development, they realize there are no rules. Parent–child interaction seems to be one negotiation after another, with each party expending enormous energy, trying or not trying to figure out how to tolerate sharing the same physical space.
>
> The problem is that parents may know intellectually that the changes accompanying young adolescents are normal and necessary for their children to develop, but coming to grips emotionally with these changes is an entirely different matter. Sooner or later, parents learn the hard lesson that the way to keep these difficulties from spiraling out of control is *not* to turn a blind eye to the more problematic dimensions of their children's development, or to disengage from their children's lives, but to become more engaged than ever—but gently, ever so gently.

It's easy to miss the signals that young adolescents send our way because the messages can change from day to day, even hour to hour. The same question might earn a smile on one occasion and make the child apoplectic the next. The conflicting responses often lead to consternation and confusion on the part of parents.

Yes, young adolescents want their parents to pay attention to them, but then again not so much. They're despondent when their parents don't show up to watch their talent show performances or their soccer games, but they'd rather that you not acknowledge them in public. Middle-grades students want their parents to remain active in their schools but not to hug them in front of their friends. The best advice is to develop a sense of humor and perspective about this look-at-me, don't-look-at-me syndrome because by the time you fully understand it, your child will have moved on to a new phase.

"Give me freedom, but care about me, too," an 8th grader from Vermont urged her parents in our survey. "Help me when I need help. Don't over-react when I make mistakes (there are many)."

A 6th grader from Kentucky asked her parents to "try to understand me more. Sink down to my level and understand what I'm going through at this age when everything is new to me."

Keeping the communication lines open with middle-grades students is essential to helping them become healthy, happy, productive adults. Many adolescents who responded to our survey said they have good relationships with their parents or other guardians and they rely on them for support.

When asked what advice they would give their parents about raising them, many adolescents gave responses similar to this 13-year-old from New Mexico:

"Nothing," she told us, "they're doing everything right."

That's not a bad assessment from children who are notoriously difficult to please.

LEAPS IN LEARNING

Adolescence is a time of intellectual curiosity and discovery when young people have a much greater capacity for complex thinking. Until recently, scientists thought that children's brain development slowed during adolescence, putting them in a sort of academic holding pattern. New, advanced research shows just the opposite. The gray matter not only expands during adolescence, it goes through one of its biggest growth spurts in puberty, particularly in the areas of the brain responsible for such functions as problem solving, reasoning, and organization.

Scientists believe that the brain changes and expands through experience. Practicing new skills, particularly when we can touch related objects or conduct experiments, solidifies the pathways to the brain's memory station. By contrast, inactivity creates a sort of mental flabbiness. Without proper stimulation, the brain begins shutting down neural pathways until the thinking passages become sluggish.

Many middle-grades teachers have grasped this new research, helping their students understand the powerful and complex machinery of the brain while showing them how to exercise it to gain maximum efficiency. For example, a teacher and counselor from Suttons Bay, Michigan, created a comprehensive unit about the workings of the human mind in which students dissected sheep brains in science class, charted data about children's preferred learning styles in math class, explored the nature of identity in literature class, built models of the brain in art class, and played neuron chain tag in physical education class.

Young adolescents enjoy movement—dancing, singing, and chanting—to help them with memorization. They prefer debating points instead of just being told to accept ideas as fact. They love conducting experiments, taking field trips, and consulting with experts. Researchers have discovered that the more active the student's involvement, such as performing a skit to demonstrate a literary or historical interpretation, the more likely the brain will learn.

"Much of what we remember for the long term comes not just from the initial instruction but from interacting with new information," veteran middle-grades teacher Rick Wormeli writes in his book *Meet Me in the Middle*. "For example, when we let students physically manipulate mixed number divisions in a unit on fractions or listen to a tape recording of a conversation in Spanish to reinforce vocabulary words, we give them the means to retrieve concepts later with far more accuracy than traditional methods such as lecturing allow."

Middle-grades students are capable of thinking abstractly about ideas instead of only being able to consider whatever is right in front of them. These emerging reasoning skills don't develop at the same pace in every child. Just as their physical maturity varies, so does their intellectual growth. For example, some adolescents are quite comfortable with the concepts of algebra in the 7th grade. For others, the light might not go on until the 8th or 9th grade.

"The brain is a snowflake because no two thoughts are exactly the same," explained a middle school student from Michigan. "Thoughts can come from nowhere and come at any time."

Young adolescents work hardest in school when the topic or task interests them, when they understand the purpose of the assignment, when they have a choice about how to convey their knowledge, and when they have a strong relationship with the teacher. It's clear that some middle-level teachers routinely use this formula for success. In the surveys collected for this book, middle-grades students recalled challenging and interesting assignments, such as the monologue they memorized and performed, the three-dimensional model of an animal cell they built, the book they wrote with "a real author," and the coast-to-coast road trip they planned for geography class.

Lisa, a 7th grader quoted in *Meet Me in the Middle*, explained the difference between a routine assignment and an engaging one: "In sixth grade, part of our history curriculum was to study the ancient civilization of the Romans. The easiest thing to do would be to tell us to read the chapter in the textbook and answer the questions at the end, but our teacher decided to be different and told each table group to take a different part of the chapter and present the information in a song. We were given a week to prepare. Our teacher was astounded by the effort we put into the project. I guess it paid off, because I can still remember the lyrics to the songs, even the one I didn't sing. Besides, I aced the test."

The arts can provide powerful ways of engaging middle-grades students as they learn about other subjects, especially when teachers integrate lessons across the curriculum. For many students, the arts help them tap into what they already know about topics, making them more receptive to new knowledge and giving them opportunities to demonstrate their understanding through written or oral performance.

The students in our survey expressed pride in their many successes in school, especially when they persisted with difficult assignments. They also shared their gratitude for teachers who showed them how, not just what, to learn.

How Students Feel About School	Girls	Boys
Most of the time, I am . . .		
Bored	42%	41%
Interested	28%	29%
Challenged	26%	21%
Confused	16%	12%
Excited	16%	11%
Overwhelmed	11%	11%

Note: Because some respondents chose more than one answer, totals do not equal 100%.
Copyright © 2003 Holly Holland and Patrick Barry

> An 11-year-old from Kentucky praised his math teacher, who "takes time off of anything just to make sure we understand what to do. And she uses examples."

> A social studies teacher from Vermont earned accolades for giving her 8th grade students new insights into the complexities of countries. "We did neat stuff like game shows with our groups about cultures and places," one student said.

> An 8th grader from Massachusetts said math was her favorite class because "the teacher made the class fun and easy to enjoy. Her teaching methods were a great part in what helped me learn."

Such examples demonstrate that adolescents can soar in school when they have the right kind of stimulation and support. Unfortunately, some middle-grades teachers don't connect well with their students—42% of those in our survey said they are frequently bored in school. People tend to dismiss such comments as meaningless complaints from restless and alienated youths. However, if we listen to them carefully, adolescents provide deep insights about what turns them off to school.

> "When the teacher stands at the front of the room and just tells us things from a textbook, I'm not learning anything," a 7th

> grader from Vermont responded in our survey. "I need hands-on things that I'm interested in."
>
> An 8th grader from Maine said she "didn't understand why we needed" to know certain lessons in math. "I know it's important but some things I don't understand what the point is. It was like they were wasting our time."
>
> "My worst class is social studies," said an 8th grader from Florida. "I don't like the teacher but I like the subject. The teacher always gets off track and repeats the same things over and over."

What these students and others are telling us is that facts have little meaning to them—and therefore won't stick in their memories—without historical context and connections to the world around them. Young adolescents learn best when they understand why dates, details, or descriptions are important to know. Teachers who convey excitement for their subjects, demonstrate relevant applications of their lessons, and provide a framework for understanding new ideas help students learn more than instructors who just regurgitate information.

One of the most important considerations for teachers of young adolescents is never to underestimate their intelligence. While they might not have the wisdom and perspective that often comes with maturity, adolescents are not empty vessels but conscious conduits of ideas and insights. Educators who recognize adolescents' vast capacity for learning and who spice their instruction with clarity and enthusiasm will be astounded by the response.

Adolescents are passionate and highly social beings who are stimulated by current events and are capable of participating in a wider universe of activities than during childhood. They seek opportunities to demonstrate their competence, to test their ideas, and to leave an imprint on the future.

Consider a few of the "greatest accomplishments" they shared in our survey:

> "Learning to read when I was younger because if I can read I can do pretty much everything."

"Getting the award for being a natural leader."

Writing "my screenplay that is 11 pages, which I plan to expand."

"Getting on the math team because I've always wanted to be on it."

"Building a go-cart that has an engine and goes 30 MPH."

"The books I write. I think they're really good and interesting and unique."

"I think I am good at bringing people together. Like when there is a fight I can help solve it. In the past I have made a couple worst enemies friends."

"Getting my first horse because I earned it myself."

"Making it on the Honor Roll one time."

"Doing a 50-mile canoe trip! 50 miles is a long way."

"Finally getting along with my mom, 'cause it's nice to be friends with her instead of arguing."

"Passing 6th grade French because I was failing all year."

"Climbing Mt. Katahdin, because I thought I would never be able to make it. And I did!"

"Getting through all the pain that has happened in my family. Stuff like that is hard to cope with at 11, 12, 13 years old."

Such achievement makes it all the more troubling that many middle-grades students are performing below their potential. Results from the National Assessment of Educational Progress (NAEP), considered the nation's report card, show that across the country only one-third of 8th graders meet the standard in reading, one-fourth of them do so in math, and a little more than one-fourth of them reach the goal in writing.

The problems are most profound among adolescents who come from poor families or are members of racial and ethnic minorities. These students usually attend segregated and overcrowded schools with a high percentage of weak and inexperienced teachers. Not surprisingly, "two-thirds or more of the students perform below the basic level on national tests," *Turning Points 2000* concluded.

"School is not a bad place to be, if you are lucky to be in one of the great schools with such high standards," an 8th grader told researchers for *The MetLife Survey of the American Teacher 2001*.

Many teachers, parents, and middle-grades students themselves do not have high expectations for learning. Most troubling, however, is that teachers tend to have the lowest expectations among the three. Some educators believe that certain groups of students are less able to achieve "because they *see* those groups of students achieving less on a daily basis."

While it is true that poverty and other family circumstances can make it more difficult for young adolescents to master challenging concepts, many students reach and exceed high academic expectations in spite of significant hardships. Excellent teachers help ensure their success. As one principal said, "We trip over our own hearts when we let these differences become excuses for not expecting that all students can achieve at very high levels."

HEALTHY HABITS

Although adolescents are old enough to make important decisions and manage bigger projects, their limited experience sometimes causes them to take chances that can leave them vulnerable to abuse and injury. Research into the workings of the human brain shows that the prefrontal cortex, the area that lies behind the forehead and directs most of our mental circuitry, is still immature in teenagers. This helps explain why young adolescents often use poor judgment, exhibit extreme emotions, rebel against authority, and take ridiculous risks.

Adolescence continues to be the time when young people first experiment with tobacco, alcohol, and illicit drugs. The good news is that such usage is declining. According to "Monitoring the Future," a national survey of 8th, 10th, and 12th graders that the U.S. Department of Health and Human Services conducts with about 44,000 students each year, 8th graders are using alcohol, tobacco, and illegal drugs at lower rates than in the past. Smoking rates have been cut in half since 1996, and alcohol use among adolescents declined by 23%.

The bad news is that the number of adolescents experimenting with these harmful substances is still too high: one-fifth of 8th graders said they drank alcohol in the last month, 15% used marijuana, and 11% smoked cigarettes, according to "Monitoring the Future."

With the dramatic physical changes in their lives, adolescents also develop the capacity to have sex and get pregnant. According to national studies, 14–20% of girls and 20–22% of boys have had sex by age 14. And every year about three million teenagers—about one-fourth of those who are sexually active—become infected with a sexually transmitted disease. Compared to the early 1990s, the age of first sexual intercourse, pregnancy, birth, and abortion rates have all declined. For those who are sexually active, more youths reported using contraception and being educated about the risks of sexually transmitted diseases than a decade ago. Nevertheless, the United States still has by far the highest teenage birth rate among the world's developed countries.

Peer pressure, heightened sexuality in the media, easy access to information on the Internet—all of these factors force adolescents to make difficult choices at a young age. Along with these stresses, moving into middle school proves troublesome to many youngsters who are accustomed to the smaller and more nurturing environments in elementary schools. For many adolescents, the transition from elementary school to a less supportive middle school environment is associated with a decline in self-esteem, both academically and socially.

Surveys from the 2000 National Longitudinal Study of Adolescent Health (conducted by university researchers and sponsored by The National Institute of Child Health and Human Development [NICHD]), involved 72,000 middle and high school students around the country, and revealed that adolescents who feel connected to their schools and enjoy academic success are much less likely to take illegal drugs, exhibit violent behavior, and engage in premarital sex. Low-achieving students and students who feel no affiliation to their school community are more likely to pursue risky behaviors, contemplate suicide, or engage in violent activities. The study determined that school performance, not family background, is the single biggest determinant of whether a young person engages in destructive behaviors.

Adolescence may be a time of confusion, risk, and vulnerability, but it is also a period of profound growth—physically, intellectually, emotionally, and socially. For many youths, it is the time when the love of learning becomes ingrained for a lifetime, that is, if schools can keep pace with their emerging capacity for creative thinking and productive service.

Up to this point, we have talked about the characteristics of children ages 10 to 14 and explained some of their strengths and challenges. We have highlighted their accomplishments and examined some of their fears. Now that we understand more about students in the middle, we are ready to explore the history and the future of their schools. In the next chapter, we will describe the critical first steps in making a commitment to a better education for all students.

❖ 2 ❖

A School of Their Own

IF YOU COULD DESIGN A GREAT MIDDLE SCHOOL, we asked adolescents in our survey, what would such a place include?

Not surprisingly, many students preferred schools with limited homework, comfortable furniture, and regular entertainment, including skateboard ramps, indoor ice skating rinks, and swimming pools with "two-piece bathing suits" allowed.

But students also shared ideas that are not only realistic but effective methods for supporting higher academic achievement and healthy emotional and physical development. Many respondents said they would like:

- A wide range of elective courses to supplement core subjects, such as math and English;
- "Good," "caring," and "fun" teachers who would inspire them to show up for class each day;
- Respectful students who would not distract them from learning;
- Challenging, interesting, and small classes where they could get some individual attention;
- Later start times for the school day so they would feel alert in class;
- Some shared courses with high school students to prepare them for life after middle school;
- Regular recess or nap time so they could recharge their physical and mental batteries; and
- Fewer rules to follow, but more consistent enforcement of the remaining decrees to eliminate unfairness.

Students also said they would do away with daily irritations—such as rude bus drivers, overweight backpacks, and small, nonexistent, or inconveniently located lockers—that affect their attitudes about school. They also stressed the importance of strong personal relationships, not just safe physical spaces, in the schools that shape their education.

> An 8th grader from Idaho said her ideal learning environment "would be a small middle school in a small town. It wouldn't be over-crowded. Everybody would get along. Nobody would be racist."

> A Massachusetts 8th grader requested "exciting teachers that the kids would like. We would have no homework at all; we would just have a lot of class work. The building wouldn't be big. It would be a nice size. The students would enjoy being in it. Our classes would be an hour long, so we can get a good amount of our studies."

> "No homework, no bullies, more experiments" defined the school wish list of a 7th grader from Florida, while a 6th grader at his school said he would like "better food, smaller classes, and have the teachers not get you in trouble if you didn't do something wrong." An 8th grader there desires "a school that has more interactive things and not so much just sitting down and listening to boring lectures, and more field trips."

> A 6th grader from Kentucky said that if he were in charge of designing a middle school, he would make it "so much fun that everybody would want to come to school on Saturdays and Sundays."

> A 7th grader from New Mexico said her ideal school "would be fun and we wouldn't have these uncomfortable medal [*sic*] desks. It would have recliners and wood tables. The cafeteria would have more workers so everyone wouldn't have to starve in line. The rooms would be big and no one would have to carry their books all day."

> An unusually organized 8th grader from Minnesota drew a detailed design of his dream middle school and listed several requirements. Under the category of "Teachers," he included four essential characteristics: "Someone who doesn't hate me. Someone who loves to experiment. A teacher who talks to us. Someone fun."

While it might not be possible to fit all of the students' requests into a single school building, adolescents have a strong sense of the characteristics and conditions that help them learn. Too bad we rarely ask for their opinions.

MUDDLED VIEWS ABOUT THE MIDDLE YEARS

For most of the 20th century, Americans have been trying to figure out what to do with children in the middle grades. Historically treated as an educational afterthought, the 6th, 7th, and 8th grades sometimes were appended to elementary schools, while other times the 7th, 8th, and 9th grades were formed into junior high schools. Many different factors prompted leaders to choose various grade configurations to accommodate students in the middle, including the availability of buildings, changes in school district enrollments, and the mandates of court-ordered desegregation plans. But the reasons rarely revolved around what was best for the children.

Beginning in the 1960s, leading educators urged the creation of true middle-level schools that would recognize the distinctive characteristics of young adolescents and set up strong programs to serve them. The middle school movement ensued because visionary and caring educators and parents understood then—and many still do today—that children ages 10 to 14 need developmentally appropriate stimulation, challenges, and support to reach their full potential. Many of the best practices in education today have roots in the middle school movement, including interdisciplinary lessons that make compelling connections across subjects and teams of students and teachers working together so they can build unity and identity within a larger school building.

In the last 30 years, communities across the country have embraced the middle school concept, switching their buildings and staffs to accommodate students in grades 6 through 8 and putting in place policies and procedures endorsed by groups such as National Middle School Association (NMSA) and the Carnegie Council on Adolescent Development. Since 1982, NMSA has distributed more than 350,000 copies of its comprehensive guide, *This We Believe*, which recommends that schools embrace 14 key characteristics, including initiating family and community partnerships and providing curriculum that is relevant, challenging, integrative, and exploratory. In 2003, NMSA introduced the third edition of the book, along with a companion book, *Research and Resources in Support of This We Believe*. Both books support the concepts described in these chapters.

By the turn of the 21st century, there were three times as many public middle schools as junior high schools and twice as many middle schools as kindergarten-through-8th-grade sites.

In the 1990s, however, when researchers examined the reasons for the generally poor performance of America's middle-grades students on national and international tests, they found that many middle schools existed in name only. Like people moving through a cafeteria line, educators had selected some items that looked appealing yet failed to choose all the items that make up the requirements for a nutritionally balanced meal.

Researchers found that many middle schools still operate like mini–high schools, with classes changing every 45 to 50 minutes, school leaders setting minimal performance standards for students, and teachers delivering passive lessons. In a 1996 study of 1,798 U.S. middle schools, for example, 90% of teachers at all grade levels primarily lectured to students instead of providing guided instruction that gives students regular opportunities to actively explore and analyze topics.

Some middle-level teachers and administrators have been trained specifically to work with young adolescents, although many other educators have not. Not all states require middle school teachers to have special training for working with children ages 10 to 14, which is why you will find some middle school teachers who specialized in elementary education and some in secondary education.

Middle-level teachers who come from elementary backgrounds often have strong nurturing skills but a limited understanding of advanced topics, particularly in math and science. On the other hand, middle school teachers who were prepared with a high school focus tend to know their subjects well but might not know how to convey topics in ways that are interesting and relevant to young adolescents.

Some middle school teachers overemphasize the emotional development of young adolescents at the expense of their academic needs, while some seek to control the students' unpredictable behaviors instead of channeling their energy and excitement through stimulating, interactive lessons.

"Even if educators understand intellectually why young adolescents behave as they do, on an emotional level they find it challenging to respond to the ups and downs of their students," Hayes Mizell writes in *Shooting for the Sun: The Message of Middle School Reform.* "It is not unusual to encounter middle school educators who are so focused on responding to students' developmental challenges, or so determined to straightjacket students' development, that they push student learning to the margins of the students' educational experiences. It is not learning, but sympathy for students or control of students that sets the school's agenda."

Leadership for effective middle schools also has been lacking in many areas because school board members and superintendents often do not understand the special needs of young adolescents and thus do not provide the necessary direction and support for the educators who are serving them. The push for greater school accountability, consistent academic standards, and annual state assessments has thrust some middle school flaws to the surface in recent years. The typical response from communities has been to reshuffle the students—rejoining the middle grades with the elementary grades in a kindergarten-through-8th-grade model, for example—instead of examining the underlying causes of low achievement.

"Until we confront those issues, all this chair-moving isn't going to make much difference," said William Schmidt, a Michigan State University professor who has conducted extensive research about American students and how they stack up against their peers around the world. "This strikes me as another one of those oversimplified solutions to a complicated problem."

The hard truth is that school leaders in many parts of the country still have not placed a priority on providing a quality education for all young adolescents. As in the past, too many people become befuddled instead of proactive when determining the proper placement for students in the middle.

That's why parent involvement is so critical in the process of building great middle-level schools. Parents are children's first teachers, and no one knows more about their strengths and weaknesses or cares more about their success. Yet research shows that parents become much less involved in their children's education when the youngsters move from elementary school to middle school—a dramatic 50% drop in school connections occurs between the 6th and 9th grades.

While the impulse to disengage during the tumultuous middle years is understandable, fight the urge. As discussed in the previous chapter, young adolescents can be mercurial messengers, sending mixed signals about whether and when they want their parents to show up at school or to ask about their classes. But that shouldn't stop you from working behind the scenes to secure a solid footing for your children as they advance through the middle grades. If you learn more about what a high-quality middle school looks like, you can help make sure that your children attend one.

A BETTER DESIGN

Beginning in the mid-1990s, several organizations that had advocated for strong middle schools developed clearer recommendations for how to make such schools a reality for all students. These groups recognized that many educators were working very hard to help young adolescents succeed in school but did not necessarily understand how all the pieces of the puzzle fit together.

For example, the publication of *Turning Points 2000* made the strategies for effective middle schools clear, consistent, and concrete. The *Turning Points 2000* design includes seven key recommendations, well-researched practices that have been found to contribute individually and collectively to the most important goal of middle-level education—*ensuring success for every student*. These recommendations are grounded in the belief that middle schools must promote academic excellence for all students, not just some, and that the important structures of the middle school movement "must be accompanied by substantial improvement in teaching and learning."

Turning Points 2000 calls for middle schools that are both excellent and equitable, that is, appropriately challenging for everyone. Such schools:

- **Teach lessons backed by rigorous standards for what students should know and be able to do,** relevant lessons that make sense to young adolescents, help them prepare for college and careers, and reflect the ways they learn best.
- **Use instructional methods that are designed to help all students achieve at high levels.** For example, instead of passively repeating information, which is the lowest form of learning, effective middle schools give students opportunities to demonstrate what they know, such as debating opposing positions, conducting original research, or teaching others new concepts.
- **Hire people who are experts in teaching young adolescents** and provide ongoing opportunities for these educators to refine their craft through targeted training. Such schools recognize that improving achievement depends on attracting and retaining expert teachers who model the lifelong learning habits they seek to instill in their students.
- **Organize for learning by paying attention to the quality of relationships among students and teachers.** Recognizing that students learn better when their teachers care about them and challenge them, effective middle schools encourage these positive encounters by breaking larger schools into smaller learning communities and providing time for adults and students to explore important topics together in depth.
- **Govern democratically, involving all school staff members in important decisions.** Such schools are proactive, not reactive, because they encourage the adults who know the children best to continually focus on strategies that will help them be successful.
- **Provide a safe and healthy school environment** by emphasizing the critical connections between a child's well-being and a child's success in school.
- **Involve parents and communities in supporting student learning and healthy development** by establishing effective two-way communication strategies to monitor and support students' schoolwork. Effective middle schools also tap community resources to supplement classroom instruction, such as providing after-school programs, career exploration, and mentors.

Turning Points 2000 argues that these seven recommendations affect one another. For example, changing the curriculum affects instruction, and changing the school's governance structure affects parent and community involvement. Ignoring the connections is like trying to reduce your utility costs by increasing the insulation but leaving cracks in the windows. The interactions among the seven elements of school improvement require everyone interested in improving middle schools to think ahead, envisioning what change in one area might mean for the others.

Major American philanthropies, such as Carnegie Corporation of New York, the Edna McConnell Clark Foundation, the W. K. Kellogg Foundation, the Lilly Endowment, and the James L. Knight Foundation, invested millions of dollars in middle school reform initiatives during the 1990s and shared their findings widely. Some of the most important research on effective middle school practices emerged during this period with the foundations' support.

Several of those philanthropies joined forces to create the National Forum to Accelerate Middle-Grades Reform in 1997. The National Forum is a network of about 60 middle school leaders across the United States who seek to expand the number of schools that have successfully implemented most of the recommended best practices and are earnestly trying to include others. Initially, the National Forum identified four exemplary middle schools that met its extensive criteria, and sent researchers to each of the sites to report on the changes taking place. Other groups, such as the Education Development Center Inc. in Newton, Massachusetts, also searched for examples of excellent middle schools, particularly those serving high percentages of students from poor families and those with learning disabilities and limited English-speaking skills.

In the next section, we will discuss what some of these exemplary middle schools are doing that other communities can emulate.

MIDDLE SCHOOLS THAT WORK

At Barren County Middle School in rural Glasgow, Kentucky, teachers constantly stress the connections among different subjects to help students make sense of new information. For example, instead of just studying the French Revolution in a social studies class, students also can make literary links to *Les Misérables*, Victor Hugo's novel about the period, and the music of the Broadway play by the same name. Other times they create outdoor poetry trails, decorating scenes that provide historical context for selected poems and dressing as historical characters who recite the poems for visitors.

"We don't just read books to learn things," one student told observers. "We work together to explore a topic."

At Barren County, teachers regularly submit to the school's governance council samples of student work—from novice to advanced levels—and the lesson plans that supported those assignments. The council, which consists of the principal and elected teacher and parent representatives, reviews the samples to find trends that can help the teachers improve their instruction. Such targeted attention has helped the school make significant gains on the state's annual tests with students from all backgrounds.

In the urban core of St. Louis, Missouri, students at Compton-Drew Investigative Learning Center (ILC) Middle School live up to the exploratory mission of this high-poverty school. Each student is a member of an investigative learning community that examines big questions about the world, such as "Why does pollution happen, and what can we do about it?" With teachers, outside experts, and their peers, students discuss topics that often span multiple subjects, conduct extensive research, then propose solutions and products that incorporate historical and futuristic data.

"On one particular day, we observed four sixth grade students . . . sprawled on the hallway floor, just outside their classrooms," researchers from the Education Development Center wrote in one report.

Two of the students are African American and two are Anglo/European, and they have a wide range of learning abilities. One of the students has specific disabilities that affect her reading, writing, information processing, and attention to learning activities. All four students are actively participating in preparing for a read-aloud performance of a West African folk tale, *He-Lion*.

They selected West Africa as a culture to research as part of a 12-week World Cultures unit. Each pod in the sixth grade selected a culture and is studying it through reading folk tales, history, and geography. The purpose of the unit, as their teacher explains it, is to "provide students with opportunities to reflect on and apply their knowledge as they write a folk tale or myth and create a game related to their culture."

Each pod will integrate all of their materials into a book at the end of the unit. This pod's performance of *He-Lion* will be one of many oral and written culminating learning activities that encourage students to understand that "folk tales are a way to give messages in a culture and that students can think about whether those messages are important for us, too."

At George Fox Middle School in Pasadena, Maryland, teachers and administrators recognize that some students need extra time to meet high standards. So instead of lowering their expectations or giving up on the students, they identify the children's weaknesses and provide targeted assistance to build those deficits into strengths. Achievement scores have risen so rapidly as a result that the principal of the high school that receives most of the students says they're the best 9th graders the staff has ever enrolled.

During the 2001–2002 school year, George Fox Middle School teachers identified 44 8th graders who had failed a class or were performing below their potential and created a small academy with three expert teachers who volunteered to work with them. The teachers organized two intensive academic classes, one integrating math and science concepts and the other connecting language arts and social studies skills, with each class lasting about two hours a day. Students can take elective classes outside the academy.

The three teachers use consistent instructional methods so the students will not be confused about their expectations, and they develop high-quality lessons that stimulate rather than bore the students. In one unit, for example, students researched weather patterns in science and geographic trends in social studies, then adopted the role of a meteorologist and prepared weather forecasts for different regions of the country, using both computer and written applications. In another unit, they prepared budgets for a fictional family and figured the family's tax returns, using math graphing and reflecting geographic variations in their financial projections. At the end of the school year, the students' families attend a celebration where the formerly struggling adolescents demonstrate their exemplary projects and skills.

George Fox Middle School has received recognition from the state because of its improving test scores, and the success of the small academy approach prompted the staff to spread the practices to other grade levels.

HOW TO ADVOCATE FOR GREAT SCHOOLS

These few examples show how effective middle schools constantly seek to bring out the best in students by paying attention to their intellectual, emotional, and physical needs. Although the described instructional practices might seem substantially different from those that most parents experienced during their middle-grades years, the assignments and projects resonate with adolescents who are maturing during a unique time in history.

At a time when technology transforms the information cycle every 18 months, students can't possibly memorize every new development in our modern society. Worksheets that ask for factual recall might help children identify the building blocks of knowledge, but they won't ensure that they know how to analyze data, conduct experiments, compare divergent points of view, and design new solutions to complex problems. Developing those critical-thinking skills depends on teachers who have a deep understanding of their subject specialties and the young adolescents they serve, educators who know how to mine the potential of each.

Parents can play a crucial role in the education of middle-grades students by expecting excellence from children and their teachers. It's not enough to say, "My child's school has high test scores," because averages can mask failures and tests can only measure selected outputs. Better questions to ask are these:

- Are all the students in my child's school performing to the best of their ability?

- Are all the teachers and administrators experts in their fields?
- Do all students feel connected to the school and have regular opportunities to celebrate their talents?
- Do all staff members expect, teach, and model ethical and responsible behaviors?
- Are all parents routinely asked for their input about their children's education?
- If the school falls short in any area, does the community agree on how to fix the problems?

"Many parents are so stressed by the demands of modern living that it is all they can do to make sure their children have completed their homework. How, then, should parents think about middle school reform? What is reasonable for them to expect of their schools?" Hayes Mizell asks. "What matters most is an accurate diagnosis of a school's problems, the selection or adaptation of experienced or research-based approaches to solving these problems, competence and persistent good faith in implementing the reforms, and carefully assessing the results over time."

THE PARENTS' PLACE

One of the best places to start building great middle schools is by ensuring that students make successful transitions to and from the middle grades. Children are much more likely to perform well in school when they feel secure and capable.

Many middle schools give incoming students opportunities to visit their campuses before classes start, offering orientation programs that typically focus on the building layout, the class schedule, and the required policies and procedures. Although these are important considerations, young adolescents have many other concerns about shifting to the middle grades, including:

- **Safety issues**—Will the 8th graders try to stuff me into lockers? Will someone hurt me on the school bus? How can I find my way around this big building?

- **Emotional issues**—Will I be able to make friends? Will my teachers embarrass me in class? What kind of music, clothes, and hairstyles do kids like at this school?
- **Academic issues**—Will I be able to handle the homework load? How do I remember assignments from four or more teachers?

In the surveys collected for this book, students also said they needed help learning how to study for tests, how to take notes during lectures or when summarizing texts, and how to manage their time and their assignments when dealing with multiple teachers during the day. Left unattended, these problems fester and can cause students to fall behind in school, leading to academic failure and recurrent misbehavior.

Many middle schools take a proactive stance with incoming students. They might place the newcomers in a study skills class, assign them to teams so they will know their teachers and peers well, and set up regular advisory sessions where staff members attend to small groups throughout the year. Other schools have come up with a range of inventive approaches for easing transitions, including:

- Surveying 5th graders about their concerns and asking middle school students to write letters in response or to lead assemblies where they discuss common issues. Some schools follow up by pairing newcomers with older students who act as their buddies during the first year of middle school.
- Setting up annual back-to-school Transition Nights where incoming 6th graders experience team-building activities, such as participating in field events and creating a giant ice cream sundae together, while their parents attend short informational sessions designed to familiarize them with the school's academic standards and safety plans.
- Training a group of involved and energetic middle school students to act as goodwill ambassadors who will look after newcomers, answer their questions, and encourage them to join clubs and teams
- Inviting new families to attend a mock middle school day where teachers and students can explain their routines

- Conducting summer sessions where new students can meet their teachers, complete sample lessons, and learn other essential skills, such as how to use the library for research, how to contact the guidance staff, and how to use a combination lock
- Creating a library of short videos that families can borrow to learn about school activities, see how teachers apply academic standards, and find out what kinds of questions will be covered on the state's tests

Whatever approaches seem most suitable, the strategies for welcoming students should be part of an intentional, comprehensive school plan and not left to chance. To that end, it is essential that middle school faculties have ongoing dialogues with their colleagues in elementary and high schools to make sure each group is aware of the academic expectations at each level and can prepare students accordingly.

Education researchers Olga Reyes and Karen Gillock suggest that schools should go through a transition process of their own to find out how they can better accommodate students instead of expecting vulnerable adolescents to conform to a system that might not be set up to serve them well. For example, many middle schools sort students by their test scores, placing some children in fast-track classes while others linger in classes emphasizing low-level tasks that don't prepare them well for high school.

The impact of these decisions can be dramatic, creating huge inequities in children's education and exacerbating the tensions during transitions. In a 1996 study, researcher Eric Anderman followed 5th graders during their transition to two different middle schools, one that emphasized strict ability grouping and one that placed students according to their motivation and learning goals. He found that students who attended the latter school had much more positive experiences and adjusted more quickly to their new surroundings.

Setting up or improving an existing middle school transition program is a good way for parents to learn about a new campus and to establish positive relationships with the staff. Don't forget the transition from middle school to high school, too. Research shows that 9th grade is a pivotal year when dropout and failure rates soar, primarily because students have weak supports for coping with challenging course work. By contrast, middle and high schools that adopt extensive transition programs experience much lower student failure rates, according to numerous studies. The best programs offer a range of activities designed to initiate students and their families into the life of the school community.

While some of the orientation strategies recommended for entering 6th graders may apply to graduating 8th graders, prospective high school students need a stronger dose of study skills and time management advice. In studies, high school students indicated that if their middle school teachers had held them more accountable for their learning and provided tougher lessons, they would have had an easier time in the 9th grade.

Entering high school students need guidance about the courses that will prepare them for college and careers. They need a realistic assessment of their learning styles so they can maximize their strengths and compensate for weaknesses. They also need their parents.

"The importance of parents being involved in their young adolescent students' transition from middle to high school can hardly be overestimated," a digest of research about effective transition methods concluded. "When parents are involved in their student's transition to high school, they tend to stay involved in their child's school experiences; and when parents are involved in their child's high school experiences, students have higher achievement, are better adjusted, and are less likely to drop out of school."

WHAT IF YOUR TIME IS LIMITED?

Many parents, particularly if they are stressed and overwhelmed with responsibilities, tend to go it alone when trying to steer their children through adolescence. Yet the reality is that they can find strength in numbers. Working with other families and with teachers, parents can build a foundation of support that will improve the quality of education for their children. While attending scheduled conferences with teachers is important and volunteering at school is a real asset, parents can do plenty to help without ever leaving their homes.

In a national survey conducted by the nonpartisan research group Public Agenda, teachers said the most important contribution parents can make is instilling strong values in their children.

"What matters most—what is absolutely indispensable, according to both teachers and parents—is what families do to shape a child's character, to promote decency, civility, integrity, and effort," Public Agenda reported in 1999.

As a Texas teacher said during one of the survey's focus groups: "Parents have to work, so I may not see them at our open houses or conferences, and we don't do bake sales. But the child has to know the parent cares. If the parents are behind them, they can succeed. If the kid knows that if they bring home a less than acceptable grade their parents are going to be all over their case, they're going to try harder. They're the ones who will come in early for tutorials or ask, 'Miss, I didn't get this question right, what can I do to improve?'"

So, ask your children about their schoolwork. Sign their agenda planners after you've checked to see that they've written down all of their assignments. Monitor their homework. And don't be reluctant to reach out independently to their teachers and respond to their invitations to talk.

At the beginning of each new term, Indiana middle school teacher Deborah Bova starts a dialogue with her students' parents by sending them a letter that asks: "In a million words or less, tell me about your child." Parents always jump at the chance to share, she said, and their responses help her know her students better from the first day of school. "I love to bond with the families by giving them the opportunity to teach me about their children."

When Bova offered this communications tip to other middle school teachers participating in a national Internet forum called MiddleWeb, her colleagues adopted the strategy and reported tremendous success.

"The kids loved it, and many parents responded," one teacher wrote about the "million words or less" request. "I took some of them to my assistant principal, and we both sat there crying over them. It was really wonderful to get info on my students directly from the parents. The responses were thoughtful, loving, funny, and extremely insightful. I feel as if I've learned more in a day than I could in a year."

An 8th grade teacher who works with a diverse population of students said 99% of the parents wrote back. Some parents who didn't speak English dictated their "million words or less" messages, which their children wrote and returned to the teacher.

"Parents and guardians seemed thrilled to be able to share what was most important about their child with me," the teacher said. "I gained invaluable insight into my students and my heart has been won over in one short week. . . . Their stories were priceless. They brought me to tears and heartfelt laughter. They made me realize in a brand new way how much most parents and guardians love their children, how much their hopes and dreams are bound up in these children whom we are entrusted with every day to teach.

"Our responsibility is great. Yet, we are not alone in this. This is the great beginning of a partnership with our parents in the education of the whole child."

Forming home–school partnerships is an important step in building great middle schools. When parents and teachers work together, they help adolescents move through the middle grades with maximum support. That foundation also makes it possible for students to excel intellectually.

In the next chapter, we look at how great middle schools focus on academic achievement.

3

Achieving Excellence

When the teacher asks for an answer, Tamika's hand[3] is usually first in the air. Her penmanship is perfect and her homework arrives neat, complete, and on time. Tamika participates in class discussions and volunteers to take the daily attendance sheet to the office. She is such a willing and dependable student that her teachers can't understand why she did so poorly on the state's annual tests at the end of her 7th grade year. Tamika performed fairly well on the multiple-choice questions. But on the parts of the exams that asked her to solve multistep problems, apply information from different subjects, or interpret lengthy reading passages, Tamika fell below grade level.

Gustavo comes to school only because his parents make him. He rarely finds anything interesting to do there, and his teachers frequently chastise him for falling asleep in class. At home, he spends his time reading a trigonometry textbook that he bought at a used book sale, building a computer from spare parts, and designing agility exercises for his pet hamsters. Gustavo's middle school doesn't have a method of formally identifying gifted students. The only accommodations that teachers make for children who can move at a faster pace is to give them extra worksheets to fill out while the rest of the class completes the regular assignment. Gustavo doesn't want to do *more* work. He wants different assignments, creative and challenging activities that will teach him something he doesn't already know.

[3] These descriptions are composites of experiences by middle-grades students.

Larry is the class clown. He's a likeable kid with a quick wit. When a teacher asks him a direct question, he usually dodges the answer by making a joke. Working with other students in a group, he volunteers to gather materials, provide the artwork, or perform other tasks that don't require him to read or write. Up to this point in his education, Larry has managed to get passing grades by listening well in class and memorizing most of what he hears. He often gets confused, though, especially with science terms. But he's afraid to ask questions because he doesn't want people to think he's stupid. The truth is that Larry has become good at faking his way through school. Now that he's in the 6th grade, he's not sure how much longer he can keep up the act. His teachers are tougher this year, and he has more of them to fool each day than he did in elementary school.

COMPLIANT, DEFIANT, HIDING OUT—middle school students present a wide range of characteristics that affect their ability to learn. Each of them has varied strengths and weaknesses as well as distinctive experiences, preferences, and interests. Yet it's important that all of them achieve in school.

Teachers have a challenging job, diagnosing each student's needs and designing lessons that will inspire every student to learn at high levels. Nevertheless, we know from extensive research and observations that the best teachers manage to reach both the brightest and the most challenged students. The problem is that the beliefs and practices that make these teachers successful have not spread throughout most schools or school systems.

"If we have teachers who can 'teach them all'—and we do—then these teachers must become our standard," members of a task force that examined middle-grades education in Louisville, Kentucky, wrote in their 2001 report to the community. "We shouldn't accept anything less."

REACHING AND TEACHING THEM ALL

Although teachers can't create individual lessons for every student, they can make learning more personal and more rigorous by offering varied methods of conveying concepts and testing understanding. Every assignment or assessment won't please every student. But when exposed to a wide range of activities that appeal to their strengths and interests, adolescents can become explorers who will find different routes to the same destination.

Educators call this instructional approach "differentiation." It's a fancy name that means moving away from the traditional one-size-fits-all method of teaching in which every student is supposed to complete the same assignment in exactly the same way to one that honors multiple means of comprehending and expressing knowledge. With differentiation, the goal shifts from asking students to compete against each other to competing against themselves, seeing how they can improve. With differentiation, teachers sometimes will vary the *content* of the lesson, sometimes the *process* by which students learn, and sometimes the *product* they use to demonstrate what they know.

Kari Sue Wehrmann, an English teacher at Hopkins West Junior High School in Minnetonka, Minnesota, uses differentiation strategies in her effort to challenge every student. She tries to motivate adolescents by tapping their interests and giving them choices whenever possible. Before she joined the middle school faculty, Wehrmann worked at a high school where students were rigidly separated into low, middle, and honors-level classes.

At the junior high school, however, she began teaching students of all abilities in the same classes because the faculty believed it was wrong to have different expectations for students based on their test scores. Wehrmann said she realized that one type of lesson would never suit all of her students.

"I could look out at my classroom and tell that some kids would get done in five minutes what other kids would take half an hour to complete and then they'd just have to sit there and wait. I thought, how awful it must be to spend your whole day that way."

After reading widely on the subject of alternative assignments and attending professional conferences about differentiation, Wehrmann initially offered choices to a few students who had demonstrated talent in writing. While she taught the rest of the class how to write a standard essay based on a novel they had read, Wehrmann let four students pursue independent projects. One student used the time to write a creative essay and later entered it in a contest. Another student focused on adding colorful details to her short stories. The third student wrote an essay comparing a book and the movie that was based on it. And the fourth student wrote historical fiction based on the lives of influential people in the Civil War.

The success of this activity gave Wehrmann the confidence to offer choices to other students. At the end of that school year, she gave every student two weeks to pursue what she called Passion Projects, conducting independent research on topics of their choosing. The only requirement was showing that they had improved their reading, writing, or public speaking skills.

Before she turned them loose, Wehrmann spent time helping students brainstorm ideas, narrow their topics, and understand the caliber of work she expected. Students wrote project proposals and revised them. Wehrmann and the students then created contracts—which they and their parents had to sign—specifying what they would learn, when they would complete the research, and how they would be evaluated.

The results were "amazing," Wehrmann said. One student demonstrated his knowledge of the history of linguistics by creating a storyboard and an audiotape for a commercial. Another student wrote a 22-page science fiction story. Wehrmann said the best work came from students who didn't shine on typical assignments.

"A lot of kids who are really high achievers are sometimes not the brightest in the class. They *play* school well," Wehrmann said. "These types of projects can sometimes freak them out. They say, 'Just tell me what to do and I'll do it.'"

For other students, the chance to demonstrate their knowledge in unconventional ways can help them excel for the first time. Wehrmann recalled one student who had learning disabilities but a genius-level IQ score. He earned only average grades in most of his classes and failed to complete many assignments.

"Once he knew that I was willing to do alternative learning concepts with students, he took off," Wehrmann said. "He did the work he should have been doing all along. It opened my eyes to his passion and what got him going. I was able to tap into that throughout the year."

Wehrmann continues to refine her differentiation strategies each year. She has found that the more choices she gives students, the harder they work and the higher they achieve. They all learn the same basic concepts—whether it's characterization in fiction or the historical context for biography—but they might read different books from the same time period and tackle assignments with varying degrees of difficulty. Sometimes she lets them choose the content of their writing when she's emphasizing a particular essay format, and sometimes she lets them choose the writing format when she's emphasizing the English content.

"One of the things I love so much about being an English teacher, I get to know the students much better because of their writing," Wehrmann said. "It makes me appreciate teens. When I hear friends or other people talk [badly] about them, saying they're hoodlums running through the mall or why would I want to be with them every day, I say, 'You've got to be kidding. Teaching 13- and 14-year-olds is incredible. It's just the best."

In the same way that actors try to tap into a character's emotions, effective teachers seek to understand a student's particular motivation for learning:

- Does she work harder when she has frequent opportunities to earn good grades? If so, the teacher can provide formal and informal assessments on a regular basis while encouraging her to find the intrinsic value in learning.
- Does he need physical outlets during the day? If so, the teacher can vary the activities to provide time for movement during class, such as conducting experiments or inviting him to physically demonstrate his knowledge of key concepts. Wehrmann often lets students "get physical" when reviewing for tests or organizing essays. They might create huge webs, using index cards and string, to show the various relationships of characters in a novel, or arrange the paragraphs of a compare/contrast essay on the floor like pieces of a puzzle.
- Will she grasp the math concepts better if she can draw them, discuss them, or write about them? Some students need to physically manipulate numbers, not just memorize them. Savvy teachers recognize that there are different ways to learn ideas, that everyone doesn't process information the same way.

Most Challenging Assignment in Middle School

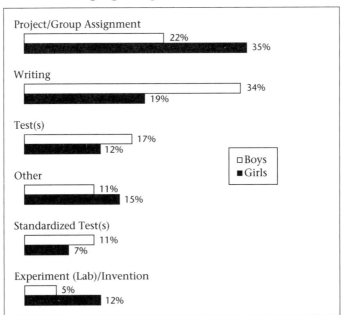

PLEASE UNDERSTAND ME

Over the years, in focus groups, surveys, and case studies, adolescents have talked openly about how they prefer to learn:

- **They need choices so even routine concepts become interesting and relevant.** In the surveys collected for this book, a Minnesota 8th grader told us her math instructor "loved to teach, knew how to teach, and made the classroom a fun place to be. She always would give us choices, whether to work in a group or separate." By contrast, the girl said, her least favorite teacher "talked in a monotone and never let us do group activities. He only taught for the money and really didn't know how to teach."
- **They need experience analyzing, applying, and adapting new information and skills.** A Kentucky 8th grader still remembers the 6th grade math/science project he did in which students had to factor the price, strength, and durability of materials when

building bridges with toothpicks. The bridges that could hold more weight at the lowest cost earned prizes. An 8th grader from Minnesota enjoyed her social studies class because "we did simulations where we kind of acted out different things that happened" in Colonial America. "One simulation was everyone got 10 M&Ms and then we were 'taxed' for having braces or wearing jeans, like the colonists were by the king [of England]."

- **They need examples of quality work so they will have tangible targets to hit.** A 7th grader from Massachusetts said her drama class connects important concepts through experience because "the teacher will base the lesson on what we have to do for homework so that we understand it. She also acts things out and uses examples." A Minnesota 8th grader said science was his favorite class because the teacher helps students understand how to be successful. "She shows us a demonstration before we do the project or lab."

- **They need opportunities to retry and revise assignments so they can profit from their mistakes.** "The class I like the most is orchestra," explained a 7th grader from New Mexico. "I like how the teacher treats us evenly. She's helped me learn if you try hard, that's all that matters." A Minnesota student said her 7th grade social studies teacher "made it feel like it was okay and you shouldn't be embarrassed to raise your hand and say, 'I don't get it.'"

- **They need an audience other than the teacher so their learning will have a purpose beyond compliance.** In Vermont, one 8th grader said he learned more from "writing a book with a real author" than any other assignment in middle school. Extending learning outside the classroom also inspired an 8th grader from Florida. For one assignment, she was able to "go to a mall and list all the stores and make a big survey and graphs about everyone."

- **They need teachers who will challenge them by building on what they know, instead of criticizing them for what they don't.** "Sometimes the things I find the most challenging are actually the most fun," said an 8th grader from Vermont. "It's harder to concentrate when I don't care about what I'm doing." In Massachusetts, a 7th grader gave her language arts teacher the ultimate praise for inspiring all students to pay attention and learn: "My teacher could make a brick interesting," she said.

All adolescents want to learn. Some of them achieve success more quickly than others do and some of them require unusual motivation, but all of them start out with the desire to do well. Several factors can throw them off course, including the limited connections they feel to their teachers and peers, the difficulty they have learning skills taught in conventional ways, and the lack of recognition they receive for their efforts.

"I never had a favorite class, I always got F's, and never got anywhere," a troubled 8th grader told us in the student surveys collected for this book. "All the classes sucked and I would often hide in the bathrooms."

Academic trauma doesn't just afflict low achievers in school. Sometimes the most able students hide their talents too. In a recent study of 100,000 middle and high school students, Cornell University professor John H. Bishop found that many adolescents underplay their intelligence because they fear being ostracized and labeled "freaks" or "nerds" by their peers. Socially popular students often apply these labels as early as the first weeks of middle school, initiating a cycle of verbal and physical abuse that can last for years for some adolescents.

Effective middle schools don't write off students who struggle, and they don't tolerate hazing of students who excel. They stress cooperation instead of competition while valuing every student's contributions. They continually set the academic bar higher, no matter where the students started, and provide enrichment and imagination to help them move ahead.

"The biggest thing is to make them see that they can be successful," said Judy Gulledge, an award-winning middle school science teacher from Norfolk, Virginia.

Before Gulledge starts teaching a new topic or skill, she probes her students' level of understanding. "I do a pre-assessment at the beginning of every unit. There's no reason to make a kid go through all the steps of a unit if he already knows it."

She might provide alternative assignments, such as an independent investigation, for students who have a head start on the material. For those at the other end, she starts by showing them that they can achieve, too.

"Something I do is to guide them through something that they can get an A or B on early on," Gulledge said. "I take them through all the steps, whether it's preparing for a test or a project. So they have the support and are putting forth the effort and steps right in front of me."

One year she taught a learning-disabled student who had failed several grades. Although the boy spoke slowly and struggled to finish his assignments on time, Gulledge noticed that he seemed to have a deep understanding of some topics during discussions. Working with a special education teacher, Gulledge spent time talking with the boy to better understand his interests and motivation. They discovered that the boy's weak physical skills made it difficult for him to write under timed conditions, so they let him put abbreviated answers on homework and tests.

"He was fifteen in the 7th grade, and all of a sudden he's getting A's and B's just because someone gave him time," Gulledge said. "He became an advocate for himself. By the time he left middle school he was in the National Junior Honor Society."

For Gulledge, the experience confirmed her belief that when teachers set high expectations for students and provide multiple ways for them to demonstrate their knowledge, adolescents rarely fail. "When you believe in them enough that they are going to be able to do something," she said, "there are very few times that kids don't believe that too."

THEIR LAST BEST CHANCE

Achieving academic excellence is not an accident. It comes from having high expectations and an intentional, consistent focus on success for every student. No one believes this is an easy job, but it is an essential one. Middle school is where students begin the serious preparation for college and careers. If they choose courses or get placed in classes and programs that do not help them progress, they may lose their last best chance to reach their full potential. Many young adolescents have already fallen behind.

In one study of urban, suburban, and rural middle schools in three U.S. states, education researcher Gerald Le Tendre found widespread curriculum tracking that placed most poor, minority, and non-native-English speakers in low-level classes that lacked depth. Because many of these students and their parents rely on teachers' advice and recommendations for course selection, they often do not understand the magnitude of the decisions made in the middle grades.

"In individual classes, students may worry greatly about grades and homework—depending on the rigor of the teacher and his or her use of homework—but overall a blasé attitude" was the normal attitude about schoolwork, LeTendre wrote. "For most of these students, 'getting into' high school was the major educational goal." Few understood that the courses they choose in school and the effort they put into homework and assignments determine whether they can go to college or pursue certain careers.

In addition, schools often make it difficult for families who are unfamiliar with the system to understand how their choices significantly affect their children's futures.

"Over the period from upper-elementary to high school, students experience several major educational decision processes," LeTendre wrote. "Beginning in 4th grade, and continuing on through high school, most U.S. students appear to be grouped by reading ability, thus receiving different curriculum. Beginning in 5th grade, in many but not all districts, students are placed into separate math classes. This placement process reoccurs every year throughout middle school."

In reality, tracking students into classes by "ability" is not a neutral, objective process. As several researchers have pointed out, poor, minority, and immigrant children are overrepresented in low-level classes. Tracking also reinforces the "bell curve view" of human intelligence that considers intelligence fixed. Research on the brain and human learning contradicts this view and confirms that our intellectual capacity can grow throughout our lives. To say we can predict a child's ability to learn at any age, whether it's 4 or 14, flies in the face of what we now know about the development of the human mind.

Setting limited expectations for learning doesn't inhibit only poor, minority, and immigrant students. When schools fail to provide challenging, engaging instruction for all students, the impact has a rippling effect on the entire community. Sometimes it takes a powerful, personal experience to make people aware that the damage done to one ultimately affects them all.

For example, each year since 1999 Jefferson County (Louisville, Kentucky) Schools Superintendent Stephen Daeschner has sent principals a list of the children in the 97,000-student district whose standardized test scores in reading fell below grade level the previous term. The roster is designed to identify children who need extra assistance—5,600 middle-grades students appeared on the list in 2002.

One year a Louisville middle school principal received a roster with 276 names on it—representing nearly one-fourth of the school's population—and sent the list to the tutoring coordinator. At the end of the day, the coordinator showed up at the principal's office with a worried expression on her face.

Did you know that *your* child is on the list, she asked?

From that point on, the principal said, she never looked at the list the same way. Instead of passing the responsibility to someone else, she took charge of analyzing the achievement data, giving teachers a personalized list of their lowest-performing students.

"I tell them, 'These are the kids you have to do back flips for,'" she said. "'These are the kids we've got to help.'"

Now teachers routinely share details of students' progress instead of waiting for the principal's questions. The principal also has developed a computerized spreadsheet to track students' participation in extracurricular activities, among other things. The greater attention to struggling students is paying off at this middle school, which the district recently recognized for reducing the achievement gap between black and white students.

School performance has to be "personalized if we want to make a difference," the principal explained.

WHAT DO THEY NEED TO KNOW?

Adolescents need models of success. They need examples of the targets they are expected to reach and step-by-step explanations of the process that will help them hit a bull's-eye. Earning a grade of A or F matters very little if students don't understand what the mark represents and can't distinguish the quality of work that produced it.

During the 1990s, many people who were troubled by the inconsistent performance of American students urged states to adopt common standards of learning. These people argued that communities should be able to expect that the graduates of every school have mastered essential skills. Up to this point, individual teachers—in some cases, entire schools and communities—had very different notions of what a 6th grader or an 8th grader should know and be able to do. What one school considered A-level work wouldn't earn more than a C or a D in others. Such irregularity hurt students when they switched schools or when they took standardized tests and discovered that they hadn't been well prepared.

The effort to take some of the guesswork out of academic expectations led every state but Iowa to adopt content standards in most subjects and grade levels. Every state but Nebraska also requires schools to test students at specific points in their education to make sure they are learning what they are supposed to know. Some of the annual state tests have high stakes attached to them. By 2008, for example, 24 states will require students to pass a specific test to graduate. In some cases, states prohibit students from advancing to the next grade level if they fail the required exams, and teachers and principals can lose their jobs if the schools' test scores don't improve. In other states, states use the information from the tests to redirect resources so schools having difficulty meeting the standards receive the most support.

Many teachers have had trouble adapting to the changes. One national study found that at every grade level, the majority of teachers believe that state testing programs have had a negative effect on their instruction. Specifically, teachers report that concerns about state testing have narrowed the methods of instruction they use with students.

On one hand, teachers generally appreciate having a clear idea of what they should focus on in class. But on the other hand, they feel overwhelmed by the number of topics and skills they are expected to cover during the school year. Many teachers also don't know what to do when students can't grasp the concepts during the time allotted. Some instructors continue to move through the lessons regardless of students' ability to keep pace. These teachers are more afraid of failing to finish the sequence than of failing their students.

"Not all standards are equal weight. As a faculty, you have to look at them and decide what's important," said Judy Gulledge, who is the recipient of numerous professional honors, including the Presidential Award for Excellence in Mathematics and Science Teaching and the Disney American Teaching Award.

Gulledge pays careful attention to Virginia's academic standards when she designs lessons, and she is mindful of the state tests that gauge students' progress, but she does not let the pressure distract her from engaging students. Too often, she said, teachers use the recommended standards as a checklist of topics that they move through at a rapid pace, forgetting the importance of making relevant connections for students.

"The standards are not the ceiling," Gulledge said. "If they shoot beyond them, you'll do fine on the tests."

As proof, she points to her students' 20-point gain on the state science test after they spent almost the entire school year researching the impact of oyster harvesting on the Chesapeake Bay. In addition to conducting a widely attended public forum on the topic, her students created an in-class AquaLab and raised 12,000 oysters that they placed on artificial oyster reefs built by the state of Virginia.

When designing units of study, Gulledge starts with essential questions or big ideas that she wants students to remember and weaves the standards through those themes.

"I want students to know that man impacts the environment, positively and negatively," she said. "I want them to understand what one organism does can affect all the others. Among that I would have [science] content standards that deal with food chains, food webs, and what happens to those. Photosynthesis and respiration would be in that unit."

To make connections to current ecological issues, Gulledge discusses the process of eutrophication, in which nutrients from wastewater end up in lakes, ponds, and streams. Ordinarily, the wastewater fertilizes algae and plants, which in turn feed fish and other wildlife. But when excessive materials, such as lawn care pesticides, end up in the waterways the algae grows too rapidly and blocks the sunlight. Eventually the waterways become "dead zones" with excessively low levels of oxygen that cause the extinction of many organisms.

"Eutrophication happens to be one little content standard in Virginia," Gulledge said. "Do I care if they remember eutrophication for twenty years? It would be great, but probably not. But I do want them to remember that the actions they do to the environment" have consequences. "I want them to remember that forever."

At Broad Meadows Middle School in Quincy, Massachusetts, language arts teacher Ron Adams takes a similar approach to academic standards. Rather than simply covering the steps to writing an effective business letter—one of the state's English standards for the middle grades—Adams uses it as the engine for a life-changing assignment that helps students mentally travel around the world and make a difference. After studying the U.S. Constitution and the Universal Declaration of Human Rights, his 7th graders investigate violations and try to "right a wrong," using their letters to persuade people to change policies and practices.

Since 1987, Adams's students have moved people to action in small and large ways, including persuading the mayor to initiate a neighborhood cleanup campaign and raising $147,000 for a Pakistani school serving children who were sold into bonded labor.

"Students want to be connected to the community and involved in making the world a better place," Adams said. "When they can use their writing to learn about and influence issues they care about, they find a purpose and an audience for their work. The curriculum becomes an extension of their lives."

SOARING IN SCHOOL

How do accomplished middle-grades teachers ensure that their instruction incorporates the critical factors of challenge, interest, and choice while also providing a clear purpose, regular practice, tangible targets, and the freedom to learn from mistakes? First, these teachers set high expectations for all students. Set the bar too low and they'll quickly lose interest. Set the bar too high without also providing the instructions and support for clearing it and they will surely fail. But when their teachers establish challenging targets, convey the belief that they are capable of reaching them, and ensure success by providing appropriate instruction and resources, adolescents rarely falter.

Second, effective middle school teachers search for connections to classwork. What are the students interested in knowing or exploring? What are they passionate about? What is happening right now in the community or the world that would help them understand this topic or issue?

Third, accomplished middle school teachers continually build trust. Learning is hard work. It takes dedication and practice. Coaches know this. They show athletes how to persist, how to try different approaches, and how to work with teammates. They help them visualize reaching a desired goal. Accomplished teachers employ similar techniques, moving students out of their comfort zones by persuading them that they can succeed at a higher level.

Finally, effective teachers routinely evaluate how well everyone is learning what was intended. Teachers should check for understanding all along the way, not just by testing students at the end of each unit. And they should use a variety of assessment methods that give students multiple means of showing what they have learned. In addition to quizzes and tests, teachers can use interviews, questionnaires, conferences, class discussions, informal observations of small groups, and projects. With each assessment, whether formal or informal, teachers look for evidence of learning. Educators Grant Wiggins and Jay McTighe contend that teachers should think of students "like juries think of the accused: innocent (of understanding) until proven guilty by a preponderance of the evidence."

The best lesson in the world is little more than a collection of ideas if it doesn't help students gain necessary skills or knowledge. Sometimes, however, the best learning occurs when teachers scrap their intended lessons for those that surface during the process of discovery.

Dr. Keen Babbage, an associate principal who also teaches social studies in Lexington, Kentucky, leads students to a deep understanding of economics concepts such as capitalism and supply and demand. His students collect mailings from credit card companies, read the fine print, and figure out how much people will owe at various interest rates. They compare prices of their favorite products in stores at different times of the year. And they research the cost of advertising on television, figuring out the best marketing strategy for products aimed at their age group.

Such lessons get students so involved in learning that they almost forget they're in school. Babbage recalled the time an 8th grader asked for more work.

"I didn't really have another project planned," said Babbage, author of *Extreme Teaching* (Scarecrow Press, 2002), but he asked the student, "What do you have in mind?"

After listening to the student's idea, Babbage agreed that the class could create magazines based on themes of their choosing. He and the students decided on the basic requirements—including the Table of Contents and a certain number of original articles, advertisements, and photographs—then devised a scoring guide that all students would follow.

"The results were spectacular, better than I could have gotten if I had made all the decisions," Babbage said. "It's important to me that they think this is fascinating. They never say that, though. What they say is, 'Dr. Babbage, this is fun.'"

John Yow, who wrote the book *Teachers: A Tribute to the Enlightened, the Exceptional, the Extraordinary,* believes that accomplished teachers inspire their students because they "possess a persistence, focus, and passion for what they do. They are enthusiastic leaders who generate sparks of discovery. The best teachers are those who make demands on their students. . . . Most importantly, every teacher, no matter how tough on the exterior, demonstrated an unconditional love for the subject matter and for the students in their classes."

Effective middle-grades teachers focus on the heart and the head, which leads to understanding, enjoyment, and high achievement. They get results with all students, whether they are like Tamika, Gustavo, or Larry.

In the next chapter, we'll look at ways in which exemplary middle schools reinforce the foundation for high achievement by establishing strong relationships with students and their families.

❖ 4 ❖

Getting to Know You

SPEND A FEW MINUTES TALKING WITH MIDDLE-GRADES STUDENTS at Vermont's Shelburne Community School and you realize right away that they have a special kind of relationship with their teachers.

"My teachers all know me really well," said Samantha, a 14-year-old 8th grader. "And so if Cynthia tells me she knows I can do something, I feel like I can, even if it's hard. It's like she's cheering me on."

Samantha's classmate, Eric, also 14, said that the relationships he has with his teachers motivate him to persist with challenges. "I really trust Joan a lot," he said. "And because of that, when she corrects me, I take it as constructive criticism. If we didn't have as good a relationship, I might think she was picking on me."

The relationships these students have with their teachers don't just make them feel better about themselves. The caring and encouragement motivate them to work harder on assignments and tests, cooperate with their classmates on projects, and understand why they should aspire to excellence.

At Shelburne, students understand that their teachers want the best for them. As a result, they learn not to be satisfied with mediocrity.

"I know they believe in me and care about how I'm doing academically," said Grace, an 11-year-old 6th grader. "And I think because of that, I try to work harder for them and end up learning more."

That's the crux of effective middle-grades education: A combination of caring and challenge that, in the end, brings out the best in young adolescents.

Samantha, Eric, and Grace are members of Alpha Team, a mixed group of 69 6th, 7th, and 8th graders who learn together in the same classrooms, address their teachers by their first names, and assist in designing the curriculum. By staying with the same classmates and teachers throughout the middle grades, they also discover each other's strengths and weaknesses and use that knowledge to help each person find a path to academic success.

The results are impressive. Between 1998 and 2000, Alpha students consistently outperformed other Shelburne students, as well as their district and state peers, on mandated state tests in math and literature.

Meanwhile, halfway across the country, Milwaukee's Hartford Avenue University School, which includes kindergarten through 8th grade, also focuses on building strong connections between students and teachers. Yet Hartford has opted to do so in a more traditional way, with students addressing teachers by their formal names and staying with the same instructor throughout the day. Spending so much of the school day together helps teachers form strong, personal bonds with each adolescent.

Principal Cynthia Ellwood credits the arrangement with dramatically increasing student achievement at the school. Science scores, for example, increased 40% the year after Hartford converted from a departmentalized setup, with students changing teachers for each subject. The achievement gains occurred despite some teachers' fears that they did not have the specialized knowledge to handle the middle-grades science curriculum.

"The teachers worked really hard and collaborated really well with each other," said Ellwood. "But in the end, at the middle school level, it's all about relationships."

The way 7th graders describe their teachers, Roxie Hentz and Erin Shaffer, supports Ellwood's claim.

"Ms. Hentz is so warm and caring, it feels good to be in her class," Matika said. "And that makes me want to learn."

Jin Sook said she's definitely learning more from Shaffer than from her 5th grade teacher, who gave out "lots of punishments. Most of the time in that class, I was really mad and I didn't try my best. But Ms. Shaffer knows me pretty well. We talk all the time. She'll help me with anything. And when I feel comfortable with a teacher, I just work harder."

For Terrance, feeling trusted and respected by his teacher encourages him to give his best effort in school. "My relationship with Ms. Shaffer is real good—she's fun, and she never yells at me, ever," he said. "When she tells me I can do something, I believe her. And when I come back and tell her I figured it out, she's always proud of me. I'm learning a lot in her class."

"IT'S LIKE SHE'S CHEERING ME ON"

Research overwhelmingly supports the views of the students at Hartford and Shelburne: When they know their teachers care about them and believe they can learn, adolescents not only put more effort into academics, they also achieve at higher levels.

Students who like and respect their teachers feel more connected to their schools. As a result, they are eager to learn. They pay attention in class, participate in discussions, and try to do their best. According to Peter Scales of the Search Institute, "Schools that nurture positive relationships among students and teachers are more likely to realize the payoff of more engaged students achieving at higher levels."

His findings echo studies of how infants bond with their parents. Babies and young children who enjoy close, trusting relationships with their parents feel secure enough to actively explore and learn about the world around them. Such relationships produce confident children who identify with their parents' values and become contributing members of society.

In much the same way, adolescents who attend nurturing schools where they form close, positive relationships with their teachers and other adults develop a sense of belonging and learn to share the school's values and goals. When they believe their teachers will support them, students also tend to take intellectual risks that help them excel. This includes signing up for the most challenging courses. In a supportive environment, students aren't afraid to make mistakes.

"If I get something wrong in Joan's class, it's no big deal," said Eric, an 8th grader on Shelburne's Alpha Team. "She doesn't make you feel stupid. She just explains it."

The same is true at Hartford in Milwaukee. "Mrs. Hentz would never put a student down because he got something wrong," said Mohammed. "She's always boosting kids up, giving them praise, noticing their effort."

"From the first day of school, she got close to us and made us excited about learning," said his classmate, Omar.

Establishing strong relationships with students also brings out the best in teachers because they feel invested in their students' success and work hard to tailor instruction to meet individual needs. Students, in turn, respond with greater interest, creating a spiral of higher-quality teaching and learning.

TURNED OFF, TUNED OUT

Unfortunately, many adolescents are not as lucky as Eric, Mohammed, Omar, and their classmates. According to Scales and other researchers, almost half of all middle and high school students are not engaged in what they're learning. This means they're probably not paying attention in class or participating wholeheartedly in class activities, let alone taking intellectual risks. They may not be doing their homework on a regular basis and probably don't care about getting good grades.

Some students tune out because the instruction and assignments don't interest them. Listening to a teacher lecture day after day or filling out worksheets full of nearly identical problems can quickly turn students off to learning. Their attention wanders. They misbehave. They neglect their schoolwork. And more importantly, they may never master the skills they will need to succeed in life.

However, Scales reports that many other students detach from school because they don't think their teachers appreciate or notice them.

"Students who believe their schools don't care about them don't care about their schools either," he said.

To be sure, some of the flagging attention occurs because students are developing a broader array of interests and becoming more independent. But Laurence Steinberg, a psychology professor at Temple

University in Philadelphia, puts more stock in what's happening at school to cause the detachment. In reviewing the results of the National Longitudinal Study of Adolescent Health, Steinberg found that while 60% of 7th graders believed their teachers cared about them, only 45% of 9th graders did. And while three-fourths of 7th graders said they felt close to people at school, only two-thirds of 9th graders did. Because no similar decline occurred in personal connections after 9th grade, Steinberg concluded that the problems start in the middle grades.

"Something important happens between 7th and 9th grade that adversely affects many students," he said.

CONNECTING WITH THEIR PEERS

Positive student–teacher relationships aren't the only bonds that effective middle schools seek to strengthen. They also pay attention to friendships students have with one another.

"The relationships students have with each other also can affect their connection to school," Scales said.

Robert William Blum, who works at the Center for Adolescent Health and Development at the University of Minnesota, is the lead author of *Improving the Odds: The Untapped Power of Schools to Improve the Health of Teens*. He agrees with Scales that strong social relationships among students help them fill positive roles in the school community. In his research, Blum found that students who had the most friends at school—including people from different ethnic, gender, and social groups—were more connected to their school than students with few, if any, friends.

Cara, an 8th grader on Shelburne's Alpha Team, put it this way: "It's harder for kids our age to concentrate when you're worrying about what other kids think of you. It's a lot easier to get out of bed in the morning and go to school if you know there are going to be some nice people there who are happy to see you walk in."

Blum also confirmed that students who feel a sense of belonging and acceptance at school learn more. "Whatever curriculum is in place will be more effective when students feel connected to school," he wrote.

At Shelburne, students participate in orientation activities, an 8th grade leadership retreat, and daily morning meetings. They elect class officers, act in an annual team play, and plan yearly team events.

"Alpha Team is kind of a community," explained Haley, a 6th grader. "Overall, everyone works well together and is happy with each other. It's a nice environment."

When students work well together, they inevitably learn more. That was the case when one group of Alpha students set up a company called ClayZee to produce and sell tea-bag holders, soap dishes, and other products made from clay. The project, part of a unit on business and economics, required students to work cooperatively as they took on the roles of managers, factory workers, and marketers.

Like their peers at Shelburne, students at Hartford said the sense of classroom community makes it easier to learn. For example, during a geometry lesson about the surface area of cylinders, the students who caught on the fastest turned around in their seats—as if it were the most natural thing in the world—to help those who were struggling.

"In our class, there's no arguing, no wasted time. Ms. Hentz is there to help us and we're there to help each other," said Omar. "We're a community. And if one of us falls, everyone falls. So we never let anyone fall."

A GOOD PLACE TO BE

Adolescents learn by observing and are quick to spot inconsistencies between what adults tell them to do and what they see the adults model in their own lives. As much as they seek to be independent, adolescents are followers who constantly pick up cues about what's acceptable in different settings. If they see or hear teachers talking disrespectfully to their colleagues, for example, they are more likely to repeat those behaviors.

The relationships among school staff members and between staff and parents also can affect student achievement. Researchers studying the Chicago Public Schools found that teachers, administrators, and other professionals who trusted each other and demonstrated respect for parents were more likely to make changes at their school that led to higher achievement than those working at schools where such trust did not exist.

The researchers, Anthony S. Bryk and Barbara Schneider, noted that at schools with high levels of trust, educators were respectful to each other. Teachers and principals listened to each other's ideas and treated each other courteously. They believed in each other's ability, valued each other's work, and cared about each other professionally and personally. As a result, teachers in such schools were willing to work together to find ways to boost learning. Likewise, Bryk and Schneider found that the schools with the highest student achievement also reported positive relationships with parents.

Consider three specific ways to build relationships that are conducive to learning: Establish and maintain a positive school climate, create small learning communities within schools, and reach out to parents.

What do we mean by a school's climate, and why is it important, particularly for students in the middle grades? A school's climate—sometimes called its culture—is made up of the values and beliefs of administrators, teachers, and students, and of the traditions that have evolved at the school over time. These values and traditions determine what people in the school think and how they act.

A school with a healthy climate or culture places a high value on positive relationships. In such schools, staff members jointly decide on their vision for the school—what it is they want to accomplish and how they plan to attain those goals. This vision becomes the blueprint that guides the staff's work.

For example, teachers at one school might seek to ensure that every student has a solid foundation in reading and mathematics by the end of 6th grade. This means that the students can comprehend different kinds of writing, from the narrative passages in novels to the more complex structures in science or social studies textbooks. Likewise, students should be able to apply math concepts that will prepare them for algebra and other higher-level courses. To accomplish this goal, the staff provides one-on-one tutoring to any 6th grader who reads or computes below grade level at the end of the first grading period. The school also provides double math and reading periods to help the students catch up and puts the strongest teachers with the struggling students, ensuring that the youngsters don't advance to the next grade level without the skills they need to succeed.

Forming a school leadership team that gives teachers and other stakeholders an authentic voice in how the school operates is one way to make collaborative thinking a regular part of the culture. How well these groups function depends on the extent to which they make decisions based on data—including test scores, observations, and other sources—instead of just using anecdotal information or listening to a few people. Collaboration often takes more time than when the principal calls all the shots, but the result is shared ownership in the decisions that ultimately determine the success or failure of students.

A school with a positive climate typically embraces respect, high expectations, and equal opportunity for all. In such schools, teachers work well together, knowing they can count on the support of the principal. They share information, learn from each other, help each other solve problems, and celebrate each other's triumphs. Teachers put students' needs first and often maintain contact with them after they have moved on to other grades.

Walk through the doors of a school with a positive climate and you will find a place where there is obvious pride in the day-to-day activities taking place. The interactions between adults in the office will be respectful and friendly. Staff members extend warm greetings, and they eagerly display students' work in the classrooms and hallways. The teacher's voice will reveal a passion for learning, deep knowledge of the topics, and respect for all students.

Principals set the tone for a positive school climate. They expect excellence from teachers and students, convey their belief that high achievement is possible, and provide the resources to ensure that it happens. They also send a strong message that they value the role that parents play in helping their children succeed in school.

At University Park Campus School, a public school in an impoverished neighborhood in Worcester, Massachusetts, with grades 7 through 12, principal Donna Rodriguez knows the name of every student and often calls them at home. She publicly celebrates their successes, including a 98% average daily attendance rate and a 100% pass rate on the state's annual test.

"She's in the classrooms all the time," said June Eressy, a 7th and 8th grade language arts teacher. "That's what helps establish the personal relationships in the school. She's tough with the kids, but she's very fair. They have so much respect for her, because they know she loves them."

SMALLER IS BETTER

In schools with positive climates, students and teachers still won't connect deeply with each other—and benefit from those connections—unless they have a chance to know each other well. That's much more likely to happen in small schools than big ones. University Park Campus School, for example, has just 215 students, and Rodriguez agrees that size is critical when building relationships with students and faculty.

"Small schools are always better," she said.

Blum, the researcher who analyzed the data from the National Longitudinal Study, said that "in smaller schools, students, teachers and school administrators all have more personal relationships with each other. . . . This is important to keeping kids engaged and a part of schools."

How small is small enough? Mary Anne Raywid and Libby Oshiyama researched high schools, but their findings seem relevant to middle schools as well. "Small enough so that people can know one another," they write. "Small enough so that individuals are missed when they are absent. Small enough so that the participation of all students is needed. Small enough so that the full faculty can sit around a table together and discuss serious questions."

Numerous studies document the advantages of schools with 600 or fewer students. In such schools, students not only learn more, they have better attendance rates and are more likely to participate in school activities. Students at small schools also have better attitudes toward school, higher self-esteem, and stronger feelings of belonging to the community. In addition, teachers working in small schools demonstrate more positive attitudes and are more likely to collaborate with each other than those working in large schools.

Small schools also tend to be safer. According to the National Longitudinal Study, students who attend schools with fewer than

1,200 students are less likely to get involved with drugs, violence, and early sexual activity than those attending bigger schools. That's because in big schools, students often become emotionally lost or physically isolated, then seek outlets in risky behaviors. Students who made headlines with their violent behavior at schools such as Columbine High School were later described as loners who felt alienated from their peers and teachers.

Despite the advantages of small schools, many adolescents attend schools that enroll more than 1,000 students. (In some big cities, school enrollments reach 2,000 or more.) At these schools, leaders need to take special steps to reorganize students and teachers into smaller groups.

Sometimes large schools can set up classes where students remain with one teacher for most of the school day. Hartford Avenue School adopted that approach in the late 1990s.

Middle-grades students made "enormous gains," said Ellwood, the principal, with reading and language arts scores rising above the national average. The staff attributes much of the improvement to stronger relationships among teachers, students, and parents.

At other schools, leaders set up schools-within-schools, "houses," or "teams" to provide students with the benefits associated with small schools. Consider Ditmas School in Brooklyn, New York, home to 1,457 6th, 7th, and 8th graders. Long plagued by low achievement, poor attendance, and serious discipline problems, Ditmas was reorganized in 1991 into four small academies run by individual governance teams. Three of the schools offer specialty programs in math, technology, and the arts. The fourth smaller academy, which has an international theme, offers bilingual support to newly arrived immigrants. Because of the changes, teachers have the freedom to work together so they can tailor classes to students' needs, and parents have become more involved in their children's education. The students, in turn, have become more engaged in their lessons. Attendance and test scores rose while discipline problems dropped.

One of the most effective ways to make schools feel smaller is by dividing students and teachers into teams. A team consists of two or more teachers who work with the same group of students and teach the core subjects of math, language arts, social studies, and science.

The students then leave the team and mingle with peers from other groups when taking electives such as art or drama.

Teams provide many of the advantages of a self-contained classroom while letting teachers specialize in just one or two subject areas. Like a neighborhood within a bustling city, a team gives a group of adolescents and teachers the chance to work together informally and formally throughout the day. Because students stay with a few teachers and attend classes with the same, relatively small group of students, they have an easier time knowing everyone well and forming strong relationships. Students also can receive individual attention from teachers.

Researchers have found that teachers and students communicate best when teams include fewer than 75 students. It's easier for teachers to set goals for their students, vary the length of class periods, and make time every day to plan together when teams are small. Teachers working in small teams are more likely to design units of instruction that link concepts from more than one subject. For example, students who are learning about the Lewis and Clark expedition in social studies might be asked to use their math skills to compute the speed at which the explorers traveled and compare it to someone making the same trip today. This instructional approach, sometimes referred to as "integrating" the curriculum, is particularly effective with middle-level students because it helps them understand the importance of learning facts and skills.

Along with the benefits for students, middle school teams enable teachers to know each other well, serving as a collaborative work group that improves their instructional practice. Researcher Linda Darling-Hammond observes that when working together on teams, teachers "fill in gaps" in one another's knowledge and "serve as sounding boards for ideas." To create the conditions for this ongoing reflection and feedback, teachers need regular opportunities to consult each other during the school day. Advocating for common planning periods in middle schools is one of the most important ways parents can support a positive school culture and effective teaching.

Another way to make big schools feel small—and help students and teachers develop strong bonds—is through the use of an advisory period during the school day. In an advisory period, a teacher, administrator, or other qualified staff member meets with a small group of students and leads discussions and other group activities covering a wide range of topics, including some chosen by the students. The topics can range from concerns about schoolwork or interpersonal issues to questions related to adolescent health or higher education.

Sidwell Friends Middle School, a private school in Washington, D.C., redesigned its advisory program in 1997. The school set up groups of 10 students who meet weekly with one teacher acting as an adviser. The groups explore different topics, such as body image, honesty, and responsibility each month. An investigation of friendship led to discussions on how to choose friends, resist peer pressure, and work through disagreements.

Such programs give students useful information about topics that are relevant to their lives as well as the chance to develop their own values. But they also provide opportunities for students to connect in a meaningful way with a caring adult.

Although we know that strong, positive relationships among students, parents, teachers, and administrators produce higher achievement, establishing these relationships is not always easy. State and federal policies, including requirements of the new No Child Left Behind Act, require schools to put more time and effort into raising standardized test scores. In some cases, this means eliminating time during the school day for elective classes, advisory periods, and common planning periods for teachers.

Money shortages also have hurt, with schools around the country eliminating elective programs, after-school activities, and, in some cases, staff positions. In many cases, class sizes have grown, making it less likely that teachers will get to know their students well. Meanwhile, as more disadvantaged and non-English speaking students enroll in schools, leaders struggle to engage families in their children's education.

Nevertheless, schools with well-developed middle-level programs continue to make strong relationships a high priority. Once in place, those relationships are difficult to break, particularly between teachers and students. In the next chapter, we examine the traits of exemplary middle-level teachers and what parents can do to support their work.

❖ 5 ❖

Teachers
Make the Difference

IN THE SURVEYS GATHERED FOR THIS BOOK, we asked middle-level students to describe their best teachers, focusing on what the instructors did to help them learn. The responses ranged from heartfelt to funny, whimsical to wise. Students said their favorite teachers:

Focus "one-on-one with every student."

"Made me feel calm, comfortable."

"Don't stand in front of the class and talk, talk, talk."

"Give us a say in what we learn."

"Made learning fun and made each student feel special."

Have "a sense of humor, but can still control the class."

Were "really involved in the subject and made me want to learn."

"Let us express ourselves and say what we think."

"Help us whenever we need it, and if [the work] is hard, find an easy way for us to understand it."

"Break down the learning procedure and really [tell] us how to do it."

"Encourage all the kids."

A student from Vermont said his French teacher "understands me well." She also was "very funny and a bit odd," he said, "but that makes her even more fun."

A 7th grader from Florida said she likes math class solely because of the teacher. "It's weird," the student said, "because math is usually my

Favorite Class in Middle School

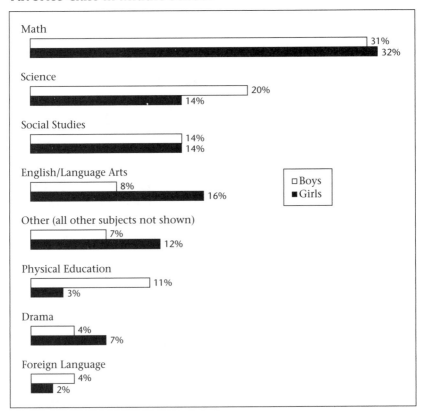

Note: Due to rounding, totals may not equal 100%
© 2003 Holly Holland and Patrick Barry

worst subject. The thing about it is, I will do much better in the class if I like the teacher."

An 8th grader from Maine praised her math teacher for taking the time to make sure everyone understood the lesson. "If we were behind," said the student, "she would make sure we caught up, without rushing us or skipping anything."

We also asked students about their *least* favorite teachers and, in the process, unearthed feelings that were equally poignant and revealing. These students described the teacher who:

Worst Class in Middle School

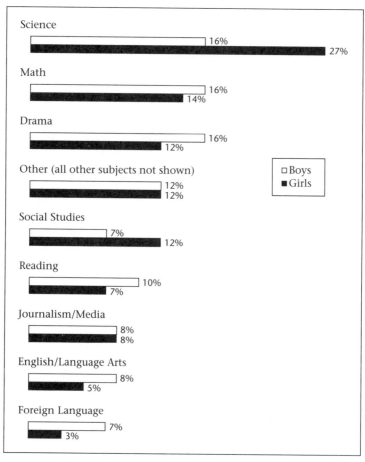

"Didn't take time to watch for good behavior . . . she just gave everyone detention."

"Has us clean out her sink, read too many *Scope* magazines, and do three pages of vocabulary a week."

"Is disrespectful . . . calling people 'stupid' is not called for."

"Is mean and talks too fast."

"Won't answer my questions."

"Just stands in the front of the room and tells us things from a textbook."

"Talked to us [as if we were] babies and unintelligent people."

"If you have the hiccups, will yell at you."

"Gives us lots of homework that she barely explains."

"Was always yelling, or talking loudly, and everything we did had to be her way. We hardly ever got any choices."

"Never used a different tone, never smiled, and was predictable."

"Yelled all the time and said we were the worst students she had ever had."

"Stuck strictly to her lectures—no fun involved."

"Was more concentrated on having fun than learning so she didn't explain things well."

"Hardly interacted with us."

In classes taught by their worst teachers, students reported feeling "confused all the time," "stressed," "nervous," "frustrated," and "bored and not challenged." Some students said they knew they were wasting their time in class and, more than once, admitted, "I'm not learning anything."

A 7th grader from New Mexico recalled that science once was one of her favorite classes. "I really used to like it," she told us. "But the teacher ruined it for me."

A Minnesota 8th grader described a teacher who committed perhaps the most egregious act of instruction—discouraging children from learning. This family and consumer science teacher "told us we were so bad that our other teachers had lost hope in us," the student revealed. "It made us lose hope in ourselves."

GREAT TEACHING = HIGH ACHIEVEMENT

The insight and eloquence of these young adolescents—often sophisticated beyond their years—relates in a powerful way the impact that

How Worst Class Differed from Favorite Class

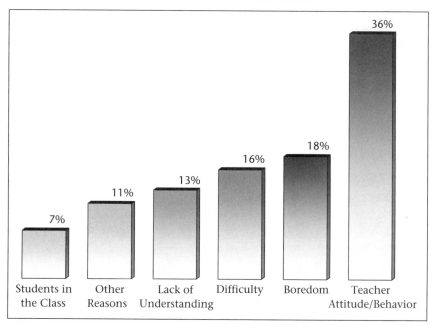

Note: Due to rounding, total does not equal 100%.
© 2003 Holly Holland and Patrick Barry

classroom teachers have on the lives and learning of their students. Sam M. Intrator, editor of *Stories of the Courage to Teach: Honoring the Teacher's Heart,* puts an irreverent spin on the point.

"It's the teachers, stupid!" writes Intrator, paraphrasing the slogan that defined the economic focus of Bill Clinton's first presidential campaign. "In other words, if schools are to be places that promote academic, social, and personal development for students, everything hinges on the presence of intelligent, passionate, caring teachers working day after day in our nation's classrooms."

As parents, many of us instinctively agree with Intrator that how much students learn depends on the effectiveness of their teachers. That's why parents "with the time and skills to do so work very hard to assure that, by hook or by crook, their children are assigned to the best teachers," writes Kati Haycock, director of the nonprofit group The Education Trust.

Principals reassure parents that their children will learn well from any of the teachers in the building. But that message doesn't resonate with the experience of many families.

"[Parents] may not always know which teachers really are the best," Haycock concludes, "but they are absolutely right in believing that their children will learn a lot from some teachers and only a little from others—even though the two teachers may be in adjacent classrooms."

When asked to rate the importance of several school reform measures, 9 out of 10 parents in a 1998 national public opinion poll said having "a well-qualified teacher in every classroom" was a very important goal. By comparison, 77% cited "a challenging curriculum" and 56% considered "reduced class size" high priorities. The top priority for parents was school safety, a topic we'll discuss in more detail in Chapter 6.

Parents' trust in the power of good teaching is well placed. In a landmark study of the link between teacher quality and student achievement, Tennessee researcher William Sanders and his colleagues ranked a group of teachers from the Knoxville area according to how well their students performed on standardized tests in reading, language, math, science, and social studies over three years. His goal: to find out which teachers had been most, and least, effective.

Over the next three years, Sanders tracked the progress of about 17,000 other students. He found that those assigned to the teachers determined to be "most effective" achieved up to 50 percentile points more—as measured by standardized tests—than those assigned to the "least effective" teachers.

Such results have led Eric Hanushek, an economist who studies student achievement at Stanford University's Hoover Institution, to estimate that over the course of an academic year students assigned to a good teacher can learn the equivalent of a full grade level more than those assigned to a poor teacher. And as Kati Haycock notes, the quality of a student's teacher can actually mean the difference between whether a student is considered "remedial" or "gifted" and gains admission to a selective college or "spends a lifetime at McDonald's."

HIRING THE BEST

Teacher quality varies greatly in American schools, in part because the profession does not attract the best students. Almost one-third of new teachers scored worse than 75% of all test-takers on their college entrance exams. Schools of education have among the lowest standards of admission of any college or university degree programs. Low pay compared to other fields is one reason that top students tend to shun teaching, as is dissatisfaction with some of the content of teacher training programs and with rigid certification requirements.

Moreover, when teachers begin working in schools, they typically find limited support and few opportunities to improve their skills. Scattered professional workshops and hurried planning periods are not sufficient to show teachers how to meet the needs of diverse learners, design challenging and engaging lessons, prepare students for state-mandated tests, and keep up with developments in their field. Rarely do teachers get the chance to observe excellent instructors, practice recommended techniques under the guidance of experienced coaches, and analyze their assignments with colleagues—strategies that research has shown to be most effective in improving instruction.

The situation is particularly dire in schools serving America's poorest children. It's no surprise that schools in impoverished areas have the highest percentages of inexperienced and marginally qualified faculty members and the most teacher turnover. In high-poverty middle schools, teachers of more than half (53%) of the classes do not have a college major in the subjects they teach. Although the new federal No Child Left Behind Act requires every classroom to have a "highly qualified" teacher by 2006, most schools have not yet figured out how to hire and keep good teachers or retrain the struggling teachers already on staff.

It's not always easy to define the qualities and characteristics that make a teacher effective. However, research tells us that at a minimum, teachers need a strong background in their subject specialties. Students in the middle grades and high school learn more when their teachers hold degrees in the subjects they teach, especially science and math.

Yet, according to the U.S. Department of Education's Schools and Staffing Survey, more than half of U.S. middle and high school students are learning English, math, science, and social studies from teachers who do not have degrees or certification in the subjects they teach. What's more, only nine states require teachers working in the middle grades to pass tests to demonstrate their subject knowledge.

Academic background alone does not prepare a person to be an effective instructor of middle-grades students. As *Turning Points 2000* made clear, teachers working in the middle grades also must understand the unique characteristics and needs of young adolescents.

Experts believe that a model middle-grades teacher preparation program would include courses on adolescent development and the philosophy of middle-grades education; opportunities to observe and spend time practice teaching in middle-grades settings; and mastery of two or more academic subjects. Yet only 51% of teacher education programs include any courses on middle-level teaching, and only 23 states currently offer middle-level teaching certification.

Principals play a critical role in shaping the staffs of middle-level schools. One of the most important jobs that school leaders have is hiring good teachers.

"In my view, the seriousness of hiring good teachers can't be overestimated," said Gary A. Burton, superintendent of the Wayland, Massachusetts Public Schools. "Employment decisions easily overshadow those regarding the number of students assigned to a class, the selection of what textbooks to use, the subject to be taught and a host of other factors that have a direct impact on a child's school experience. These are significant variables, but all pale in comparison to whom we allow to teach our children."

Denise Levigne, principal at East Side Middle School in New York City, said she looks for experienced teachers who know what they are getting into when they walk into a middle-grades classroom. "You really have to love kids of this age level."

Mike McCarthy, principal of King Middle School in Portland, Maine, looks for teachers with a sense of humor and commitment to the community. But McCarthy also tries to determine if applicants buy into the school's mission. "Do they sense that this is a place where all kids can learn?" he asks. "Will they have an understanding of the kids we have here?"

When Cynthia Ellwood, principal of Milwaukee's Hartford Avenue University School, interviews someone for a teaching job, she asks questions designed to learn about their teaching and classroom management styles. "I want to hear about ways they've collaborated with other teachers," Ellwood said. "I ask about how they've handled discipline problems."

Ask yourself whether your child's principal is doing an effective job of hiring and supporting teachers. What are the staff's qualifications? Are children excited about learning in their classrooms? Do the teachers enjoy working with young adolescents and understand their academic and emotional needs? Have they tried to identify your child's individual strengths, weaknesses, and areas of interest? Are they interested in talking with you about your child's progress? Are they positive, enthusiastic individuals who exude a high level of energy? Do they collaborate with their colleagues and seem open to new ideas?

Recruiting and hiring effective teachers is just the first step in the process of building a high-quality staff. With up to 50% of teachers in some U.S. districts leaving the profession within 5 years, schools also must do a better job of keeping their best instructors.

A growing number of schools have set up special programs for new teachers aimed at successfully "inducting" them into the profession. Such programs guide beginning teachers through the first few weeks of school and then offer ongoing support during their first few years on the job.

Induction programs typically match new teachers with experienced, successful teachers working in the same school who act as coaches or mentors. The coaches and mentors observe the new teachers while they teach, then meet with them on a regular basis to help them plan and evaluate the effectiveness of their lessons, improve teaching techniques, and solve problems. In short, the best coaches and mentors draw on their own experiences to help new teachers put what they've learned in their college courses to practical use in the classroom.

Induction programs, while making it more likely that teachers will succeed in the classroom, also increase the chances that new teachers will stay in the profession. In the Lafourche Parish Public Schools in

Thibodaux, Louisiana, school officials say an induction program begun in 1996 helped reduce the annual turnover rate from 51% to 7%. That's a significant change, considering how much time and effort school officials spend recruiting, hiring, and training new teachers. One study estimated that teacher turnover costs the state of Texas $329 million to $1.5 billion a year. Each time a teacher leaves, school districts spend about 20% of the former instructor's salary recruiting and hiring a replacement.

Schools in Fairfax County, Virginia, developed the "Great Beginnings" induction program, which brings small groups of new teachers together for a 3-day summer institute led by two experienced teachers who serve as their coaches. During the institute, new teachers learn how to set up their classrooms, design effective discipline strategies, and develop engaging lessons for the first few weeks of school. The induction program also supports teachers throughout their first 3 years on the job.

In 1989, when James Dallas began teaching in the school district, "New teachers didn't get much help. I was overwhelmed, and remember spending a lot of time in my classroom in the evenings and on weekends trying to figure things out on my own. Teachers were isolated, and so we were less collegial, less unified. It was more cutthroat, and not much fun."

These days, by contrast, Dallas said, "Working together and sharing are second nature here. I never hear teachers in the teachers' lounge whining about their jobs or talking about kids in a negative way. Instead, they talk about the things they're doing that work and urge each other to 'Try this. Try that.'"

TEACHERS AS LIFELONG LEARNERS

New teachers are not the only school staff members who need support. Teachers with all levels of experience must improve their skills. Although most middle schools offer continuing education for teachers, the opportunities tend to be limited to short workshops or classes offered during the summer, after school, or on specially designated days during the school year when students have the day off. In many cases, these sessions are one-shot workshops covering a specific skill, such as how to teach descriptive writing or keep students on task.

Numerous studies, as well as teachers' own experiences, have found these quick, introductory sessions with limited follow-through to be ineffective. Many teachers acknowledge putting the materials they receive at such workshops up on a shelf, never to be looked at again.

If professional development is to have value, to improve instruction and learning, it must be linked to student achievement and focused on results. Teachers on a team might meet to review the work students produced during a particular lesson or unit, analyzing the work for evidence of understanding and using that information to plan follow-up instruction. Math teachers from several schools might get together to analyze a district's standardized test scores, determine why math achievement declined, and propose specific solutions. After using the suggested strategies in their classrooms for several months, the teachers would reconvene to evaluate their efforts.

Other promising practices include giving teachers the time and training to develop their own curriculum, reflect on the content of their lessons, analyze the effectiveness of their teaching strategies, and conduct their own educational research. Whatever form professional development takes, it is most effective in changing teaching practices and improving learning when it is built into the daily lives of teachers, as part of "the way we do things around here."

Schools that engage in ongoing professional development make choices that allow educators to devote focused time to improving their craft. Admittedly, effective professional development may be expensive and time-consuming. Schools must pay teachers for the extra hours they work collaboratively or pay for substitutes when the training sessions are held during the school day. Although some parents question the value of these choices and are inconvenienced when schools release students early, money spent on teacher education is "likely to do more for raising student achievement than investments in other kinds of school reforms," writes Michael deCourcy Hinds in *Teaching as a Clinical Profession: A New Challenge for Education*, a report for the Carnegie Corporation of New York. And, as described in *Turning Points 2000*, "a study of more than a thousand school districts concluded that every additional dollar spent on highly qualified teachers netted greater improvements in student achievement than did any other use of school resources."

WHAT PARENTS CAN DO

Recruiting, retaining, and supporting excellent teachers is critical to the mission of good middle-level schools. However, without the support of parents, even the best teachers will be seriously restrained.

There are many ways parents can show their support for good teaching, such as attending a school board meeting to protest budget cuts that target staff development and sending their children to school ready to learn.

Students also benefit when parents enter into positive, ongoing partnerships with their children's teachers, partnerships characterized by mutual respect in which parents and teachers share similar expectations for children. Such partnerships are built on strong parent-teacher communications that begin early in the school year and include both formal and informal meetings. Teachers should keep in touch with parents through regular newsletters, e-mail, and phone calls. In turn, parents should share how their children are responding—both positively and negatively—to the teacher's lessons.

Many parents mistakenly believe that by the time young adolescents reach the middle grades they neither want nor need their parents involved in school. But as students told us in the surveys for this book, they appreciate it when their parents show an interest in their education by asking them about their school activities, supervising their homework, or simply telling them that they care.

What are some ways that parents help?

"My parents always encourage me to get my grades up, and my teacher has very high expectations," said an 8th grader from Maine.

A 7th grader from Massachusetts said he knows his parents care about his education "because I hear them talking about my future."

A Minnesota 8th grader said busy schedules at home never keep her parents from showing their concern for her education. "When my dad is traveling, I call him and he helps me with my math," she said. "And my mom helps with the rest of my homework."

For a group of 6th graders in Kentucky, the notable signs of interest from their parents included "making sure I am at school everyday," "making me read every night," and "coming to every school conference and doing homework with me." One 7th grader drew lessons from her mother's negative inspiration: "My mom tells me that she don't want me to follow the same footsteps she did," while another 7th grader acknowledged that her parents' pestering had made a firm impression: "They always ask, 'How was school?' every single freakin' day."

Effective middle-level schools welcome and encourage parent involvement, which fosters trust and mutual respect. At such schools, the principal and teachers keep parents well informed, not only about individual student progress, but also school policies and practices. School leaders strive to know parents well, make them feel comfortable in the building, and suggest specific ways they can guide their children's education, both at home and at school.

Many middle schools recruit parents to serve on school leadership teams and make decisions about how schools operate. In these roles, parents help shape school policies and interview candidates for teaching and administrative positions.

To have a lasting, widespread impact on the school, parents can use these roles to improve teacher quality, suggests William Miles, director of policy and programs for the Public Education Network, a national organization of independent, community-based advocacy groups working to improve public schools. For example, in schools with a few effective and sought-after teachers, parents could ask how the principal intends to share their strategies with other faculty members. If the school has a high rate of turnover among the staff, parents can ask the principal why so many teachers are leaving. And in years when there is an unusually high number of new teachers at the school, parents can find out what the principal plans to do to support them in their first few months on the job.

"Asking good questions is a great way for parents to get information and learn about what good teaching involves," Miles said. "It's a mechanism that lets parents engage in long-term, serious inquiry about teaching without being threatening, accusatory or demanding. Yet, it sends the message that parents are going to hold the professionals in the building accountable for their children's learning."

Parents and other community activists across the country are involved in other, more formal efforts to improve teaching. A 3-year project in West Virginia, for example, brings middle and high school students together with their parents, community leaders, school officials, and legislators in each of the state's 55 counties. Their discussions focus on how they can find and keep caring, effective teachers in every classroom.

Early results have been promising, said Hazel Palmer, president and chief executive officer of the Education Alliance, which is directing the teacher quality initiative. In the Wood County Public Schools, for example, students and parents now receive information at the beginning of the year outlining course objectives for each class. Parents and students are also helping to evaluate teachers. Trained evaluators oversee the process, which takes into account information gathered in family interviews and surveys.

In other efforts:

- Parents in Philadelphia persuaded schools to provide more support for new teachers. A pilot program lets new teachers observe master teachers, attend special classes, and work with coaches.
- In Chicago's North Lawndale neighborhood, parents and community leaders working with the Association of Community Organizations for Reform Now (ACORN) took steps to combat the high number of teacher vacancies in the area's 26 schools. The group collected data and then appeared before the local board of education three times during the 1999–2000 school year to stress the importance of hiring qualified, full-time

teachers for every classroom. The activists also helped officials recruit new teachers by organizing a job fair in the neighborhood that included a tour of the schools. The effort paid off. The following year, schools opened with a full complement of teachers. The same group also organized summer institutes for new teachers and persuaded school officials to provide mentors for new teachers.

- In the South Bronx, community members persuaded state legislators, municipal leaders, and school officials to commit to a school improvement plan that includes qualified teachers for all students.

These examples demonstrate that parents can make a positive difference in their children's middle schools. It's up to all of us to ensure that every student has a qualified, committed, and effective teacher in all subjects. Our children deserve no less.

Now let's turn to another area close to every parent's heart—school safety.

❖ 6 ❖

Safe Schools

"REMEMBER, BOYS AND GIRLS," 2nd grade teacher Ann Pulito tells her pupils every day, "my most important job is to keep you safe while you are in school."

The first time Priscilla heard that message during a visit to Pulito's Shorewood, Wisconsin, classroom, she was immensely grateful. Although she wanted her son, Casey, to learn a lot from Pulito, Priscilla also wanted him to be safe while he was away from home

At the time, shootings at middle and high schools around the country seemed to regularly lead the news, and school safety was a hot topic nationwide. In working with 2nd graders, Pulito was more focused on curbing horseplay at the drinking fountain than preventing gunfire in the cafeteria, but Priscilla found it reassuring to know that her son's teacher put the highest priority on the children's physical safety.

In the fall of 2003, as Casey moved to the middle grades, Priscilla felt the same way about the importance of balancing safety and scholarship in school. As she thought back to Pulito's reassuring words, she was mindful of the broader implications of the teacher's message: Students learn more when they are secure in their surroundings.

In fact, researcher Eric Jensen, author of *Teaching with the Brain in Mind*, said "excess stress and threat in the school environment may be the single greatest contributor to impaired academic learning."

SCHOOLS ARE SAFE

Despite tragic and highly publicized shootings such as those in Pearl, Mississippi, and Littleton, Colorado, schools are among the safest places for children. According to the Justice Policy Institute, 99% of children's deaths occur away from school. U.S. Census Bureau statistics show that a youth is twice as likely to be the victim of a violent crime at or near home than at school. The risks for injury in a store, park, or parking lot are four times greater than in school.

Specifically, data released by the National Center for Education Statistics in 2000 revealed that 90% of all schools nationwide reported no serious crime. And in a 1999 New York Times/CBS News poll, 87% of students 13 to 17 said they believed their schools to be safe.

That research is consistent with our findings—72% of the middle-grades students surveyed for this book said they feel safe in school—although the lower percentage in our poll points to pockets of problems in middle schools compared to schools overall. Students told us that having positive relationships with teachers and peers is key, which supports the recommendations for effective middle schools that we've detailed in previous chapters. Among those students who feel safe, for example, 40% cited support from teachers, principals, and friends. Specifically, they noted that:

> "My teachers care."
>
> "There are grownups everywhere."
>
> "There are good principals."
>
> "We have a cop and a counselor."
>
> "Everybody is friendly."
>
> "I know everyone."
>
> "I do feel safe. I just trust every teacher."
>
> "I have good friends that will take up for me."
>
> "Yes, they are people who care about you, not like my old school that they don't care what you do."
>
> "I usually get along with people so there's no reason for me to feel unsafe."
>
> "I know that my teachers love me and they wouldn't let nothing happen to me."

Do You Feel Safe in School?

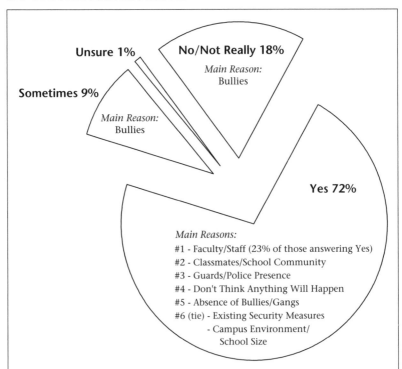

Unsure 1%

No/Not Really 18%
Main Reason:
Bullies

Sometimes 9%

Main Reason:
Bullies

Yes 72%

Main Reasons:
#1 - Faculty/Staff (23% of those answering Yes)
#2 - Classmates/School Community
#3 - Guards/Police Presence
#4 - Don't Think Anything Will Happen
#5 - Absence of Bullies/Gangs
#6 (tie) - Existing Security Measures
            - Campus Environment/
              School Size

REALITY VERSUS PERCEPTION

Of course, not all the data on school safety are positive. Too many adolescents observe or suffer from abuse, both physically and emotionally, during school hours. In a national poll of teens 14 to 17 years old conducted in 2000 by the Discovery Channel and *TIME* magazine, just over half (51%) said they had been verbally insulted or threatened at school during the previous year. And 14% of a national sample of 8th graders polled in 1996 by the Educational Testing Service described physical conflicts as a "moderate" or "serious" problem in their schools.

In the surveys collected for this book, 27% of middle-grades students said they feel insecure in school on a regular or occasional basis. Some of their hesitation had more to do with concerns about nation-

What My School Could Do to Make Me Feel Safer	Girls	Boys
Nothing	50%	38%
Add Security Measures (e.g., surveillance cameras, locks)	22%	25%
Improve Policy/Enforcement (incl. Get Rid of Bullies)	15%	19%
Have Greater Guard/Police Presence	6%	13%
Other	6%	5%
Educate Kids About Cruelty	2%	1%

Note: Due to rounding, totals do not equal 100%.
Copyright © 2003 Holly Holland and Patrick Barry

al and global events than with what was actually happening in their communities. For example, one-fourth of the students who said they didn't feel safe in school attributed their anxiety to a pessimistic view of conditions in American society.

"What happened at Columbine High School still scares me," admitted an 8th grader from Vermont.

"This is life," said an 8th grader from Maine. "Anything is possible."

At the same time, many adolescents can trace their insecurities to specific behaviors and conditions at their schools. Bullying was the major reason that both boys and girls felt uneasy in school. Large percentages of girls also feared the presence of gangs, in-class fighting, and unlocked doors that provide easy access to intruders. Whether they perceived indifference from adults or hostility from their classmates, some students said they are perpetually on alert for trouble because:

> "A lot of the cool kids hate me."
>
> "A lot of people here like to fight and . . . the next day they may pull out a gun!"
>
> "I've seen people get beat up."
>
> "A lot of people cuss and do bad stuff."
>
> "There are too [many] gangs that purposely make fun of people [of] different races."

"People are cruel."

"Anybody can come in."

"In the bathrooms I don't feel safe because of their design."

"I know someone who has a gun here."

"There are bullies at every corner."

"When people hit me, teachers don't see."

"Teachers don't do anything when fights appear."

BATTLING BULLYS

To be sure, the causes of school violence are complex. But young adolescents and teens say they believe most of the violence they observe and encounter stems from a lack of civility—kids not respecting each other. Students in 5th through 12th grades surveyed by the Families and Work Institute and The Colorado Trust told researchers they consider cruel putdowns and rejections "emotional violence" that they believe triggers more extreme and aggressive behavior.

Much of that aggressive behavior takes the form of bullying, which the National Association of School Psychologists says affects about five million elementary and middle school students in the United States. Bullying, which is most likely to occur during the middle-grades years, can include teasing and verbal threats, extortion, assault, theft, sexual harassment, and social isolation.

While crimes on school campuses decreased in several categories by about 50% from 1992 to 2000—with the biggest reductions occurring in the middle grades—the National Crime Prevention Council reports that the proportion of youths seeing bullying at least once a day rose from 37% in 2001 to 61% in 2002. Researchers have found that school bullying affects about one third of middle-grades students, with boys and girls each assuming the roles of victims and perpetrators. Forty percent of 12-to-15-year-olds said they want more information about how to handle bullying and other kinds of harassment, according to a 2001 study by the Kaiser Family Foundation.

Researchers have found that many bullies were once victims who received little assistance from adults and consequently learned that it was better to attack than be attacked. Other bullies act out in response to rejection by their peers.

The typical adult response to bullying has changed dramatically in recent years. Long considered a rite of childhood, bullying now is viewed as a serious problem that can have long-term effects on the social, psychological, and academic development of both the victims and the bullies.

In early 2003, the National Crime Prevention Council released a survey showing that bullying is "the terrorist threat that most frightens America's teenagers and interferes with their education." Says former school administrator James E. Copple, now vice president of public policy for the National Crime Prevention Council, "The impact of bullying on a school climate can be toxic. Bystanders experience fear, discomfort, guilt, and helplessness that poison the learning atmosphere even more extensively."

KEEPING KIDS SAFE

The good news is that many of the traits of effective middle-grades schools that we've already examined promote environments in which young adolescents tend to be safe from bullying and other kinds of physical and emotional violence. Consider:

- In their 1998 study of adolescent health, researchers at the Center for Adolescent Health and Development at the University of Minnesota concluded that the personal connections that students make in school become "a powerful protective factor" for them. Specifically, they found that students with strong ties to their schools were less likely to use alcohol and illegal drugs, engage in violent or deviant behavior, become pregnant, or experience emotional distress.
- According to the U.S. Department of Education, students feel more secure when their large schools are divided into "families" or "schools within schools."

- In Kansas, researchers found that students were more likely to feel safe in school if everyone in the building knew each other well. Students said they felt safer just by seeing their principal in the halls talking with students, working with them on school activities, and helping them with their problems. One student praised a principal for "mak[ing] us feel comfortable, which is a sign of safety and trust."

Effective middle schools also take a proactive approach to preventing bullying and other aggressive behaviors. Victims who in the past were told to just "toughen up" or "ignore" their tormentors now learn how to report the problem. And the bullies, once dismissed as bad apples who would eventually outgrow their aggression, receive discipline and counseling to help them identify the reasons behind their cruel behaviors.

The U.S. Department of Education (www.ed.gov) and other organizations have compiled information about effective, research-based antibullying strategies and model programs for schools and youth groups.

For example, the National School Safety Center recommends that schools focus on lower-level incidents, such as putdowns and trash talk, before they escalate to more dangerous incidents such as bullying, fighting, hate crimes, and murder.

At McCormick Middle School in McCormick, South Carolina, staff members worked for 18 months with the University of South Carolina's Institute for Families in Society to find ways to reduce bullying. Staff training and classroom discussions designed to help teachers and students learn how to recognize and respond to bullying reduced the number of students who reported being bullied from 50% to 25%.

In effective middle schools, adults also involve students in the discipline process to seek their ideas and to help them understand the consequences of their actions. By asking for their input and support, teachers and administrators also tap into adolescents' emerging interest in issues of freedom and responsibility. By the time they reach the middle grades, young adolescents generally are mature enough to reflect on their peer culture and to change it, if necessary. When students participate in the process of coming up with school and classroom rules, they also will be more inclined to obey them.

Particularly effective at the middle-grades level are peer mediation and conflict resolution programs that give adolescents a chance to solve their own problems. A program developed by the National Center for Conflict Resolution Education trains students in grades 6 to 12 to mediate disputes between students. The student mediators learn about the origins of conflict and how to solve differences peaceably. The mediator might ask the students involved in a fight to think about how each person contributed to the dispute, then to suggest ways they could resolve it. The program has reduced antisocial and violent behaviors by 19% at urban middle schools.

CELEBRATE DIVERSITY

Another preventive strategy is creating a culture of acceptance and appreciation in which students learn to treat each other with respect. In such an environment, all adolescents, not just popular and athletic students, get opportunities to shine, to demonstrate their special skills and talents, and to gain recognition and confidence. School newsletters, school assemblies, and school pep rallies celebrate the accomplishments of a variety of students, sending the message that all children are valued.

In seeking to create such an environment, school officials must make a special effort to ensure that students of all races and cultures thrive. That means eliminating all forms of racial discrimination and stereotyping as well as inequities for minority-group adolescents, such as "tracking" or grouping students into high-, average-, or low-level classes according to their perceived academic ability. This practice discriminates against minority youth, who for decades have been disproportionately assigned to lower-level classes.

In addition, schools must find ways to celebrate racial and cultural diversity. Effective middle schools include ongoing lessons and activities about a wide variety of ethnic groups. Such lessons broaden students' knowledge and set the stage for spontaneous conversations between students of all racial and ethnic backgrounds, which in turn leads to better understanding, acceptance, and appreciation of each other's differences.

These preventive efforts are critical. Among middle and high school students, 12% reported being targets of hate-related words or seeing hate-related graffiti in their schools based on race, religion, ethnicity, disability, gender, or sexual orientation.

"An environment in which students are confronted with discriminatory behavior creates a climate of hostility that is not conducive to learning," noted the National Center for Education Statistics and the Bureau of Justice Statistics in their report, *Indicators of School Crime and Safety 2002.*

Parents play an important role in preventing bullying and other forms of harassment. To start, they have a responsibility to teach their children not to bully others.

"It starts at home. If you get knocked in the head at home, it's nothing to come to school and knock somebody in the head," one student noted in a 2000 study on youth violence by the National Association of Attorneys General.

Parents also should be alert for any signs that their children are being bullied. Some signs include complaints about going to school, declining grades, unexplained injuries, trouble sleeping, or depression. If you suspect trouble, talk to your child's teachers and principal and seek appropriate action.

WHAT HAPPENS AFTER SCHOOL

At many middle schools, the task of keeping students safe extends beyond the regular school day. Increasingly, school and community leaders are being asked to fill the unsupervised time after school with meaningful extracurricular and academic activities. About 15 million children return to empty houses each afternoon where, unsupervised, they are prone to get involved in risky behaviors. The number of violent crimes committed by juveniles nationwide peaks between 3:00 P.M. and 4:00 P.M. on school days. And juveniles are at the highest risk of being the victim of a violent crime in the 4 hours immediately following the end of the school day than at any other time.

While unsupervised youths usually spend the after-school hours watching television or playing video games, high-achieving students spend at least 20 hours per week taking part in formal or informal learning away from school. Educational researcher Reginald Clark found that students who participate in organized activities in the presence of coaches and other adult leaders also have better attendance, fewer discipline problems, and higher self-esteem than their peers who spend their after-school hours unsupervised.

In Chicago's Logan Square neighborhood, for example, a study by University of Chicago researchers found that student test scores increased and parents' attitudes about their children's schools improved because of after-school programs at six area schools serving more than 2,000 children and adults. Students who stay after school get help with their homework and take enrichment classes in subjects such as theater, martial arts, and music. Adults can take classes in English as a Second Language and study for a General Equivalency Diploma.

Public support for after-school programs is strong, with 94% of those surveyed saying they want after-school programs and are willing to use federal and state funds to pay for them. Yet, research also shows that only 29% of young adolescents nationwide have a chance to take part in such programs.

There are efforts under way to change that. In North Carolina, the Support Our Schools Program (SOS), a community-based after-school initiative, provides high-quality after-school activities for middle-grades students. The program links students with adults who help with homework, organize clubs, and coach athletic teams.

The program, begun in 1994, currently serves 23,000 youths at more than 240 sites throughout the state. Officials say that 40% of the students in the program have fewer absences and suspensions now than before they joined. And at least 37% of the participants have raised their grade point averages since they started.

STAYING INVOLVED

Schools are under pressure to keep adolescents safe, and many middle-grades educators are rising to the challenge. Yet parents must resist the temptation to leave the task entirely in the hands of educators. As we've said before, while young adolescents are beginning to stretch their wings and demand greater independence, they still want and need their parents' guidance and support.

Consider the results of a 1993 survey of teens by the Horatio Alger Association, an organization that provides scholarships and mentoring to needy students. Nearly 75% of those polled—including adolescents as young as 14—said they get along "very well" or "extremely well" with their parents. In addition, many teens said they wanted to spend more time with their families and ranked family members higher than entertainers or athletes when it came to identifying positive role models.

At a time of increasing concern about children's health and safety, you can be sure that the time and effort you spend with them will pay off, both in terms of their physical and mental well-being and their academic achievement. Working closely with your children's middle schools is an excellent way to keep them surrounded by caring and capable adults. We explore specific strategies for effective home–school partnerships in Chapter 7.

❖ 7 ❖

Leadership for Learning

WHAT IS THE JOB OF A MIDDLE SCHOOL PRINCIPAL? For some, she is the "voice" of authority, the person who makes morning announcements on the school's intercom system or calls everyone to attention during an assembly. For some, he is the person whose office visits with students symbolize punishment for misbehavior. And for others, she is the person who greets them in the hall during class changes, circulates among their tables in the cafeteria, and asks about their lessons, their career interests, and their after-school activities.

While all of these views may be accurate, they don't capture the complexity of a modern middle school principal's role. Today's principals must be instructional leaders as well as school managers. In addition to operating what amounts to a multimillion-dollar business, supervising bus and class schedules, and hiring and firing staff, principals must set high standards of learning for everyone in the school building, both children and adults. They must be able to recognize effective instruction and provide ongoing training and support so all teachers can provide it. They must be savvy about using test scores and other sources of data to target school improvements. They also must tap community resources, ensuring that students and teachers have regular access to the best minds and materials available.

The principal sets the school's tone and cultivates its culture. He or she determines what is valued in the school, whether only some students get the best teachers and the most acclaim or whether all students get the chance to excel and gain recognition for their accomplishments.

"I have come to believe that the principal is the most instrumental person in education," said Michelle Pedigo, the former principal of

Kentucky's Barren County Middle School, one of the first schools in the nation to be named a "School to Watch" by the National Forum to Accelerate Middle-Grades Reform.

"It is [principal] leadership that determines the level at which the school embraces opportunities for students. . . . It doesn't mean that principals don't deal with administrative issues, but when they do, they look at what will support student achievement."

One of the least appreciated aspects of the principal's job is working with students' families. While research confirms the importance of effective family–school partnerships in building excellent schools and the federal government requires schools to promote such collaborations, few principals have a good grasp of how to bring families fully into the life of the school community.

"Up until now, involvement of parents has been mainly a matter of luck and accident," acknowledges Joan Epstein, director of the Center on School, Family, and Community Partnerships at Johns Hopkins University.

Notes Ellen Yaffe, director of the Parent Alliance for School Standards (PASS), an advocacy group formed in 1996 to help middle school families work with the San Diego City Schools: "I think middle school is a very tough nut to crack, who's invited in under the tent. It's more rare than I'd like to admit that parents are in the center ring. We've found that parent involvement is much more on the fringe, as it relates to student achievement."

Research has demonstrated that democratically run schools are more effective than those relying on traditional lines of authority. At the same time, collaboration is only one part of effective middle schools. The most progress occurs when everyone in the school community commits to practicing democratic leadership while simultaneously improving instruction. The more people have invested in the outcomes of school decisions, the more they will work to support them.

Studies of leadership in schools with high student achievement have found common characteristics of principals, including their ability to make teaching and learning the focus of all discussions and their willingness to share power with teachers and parents. School leadership teams that include representatives from all sectors of the school population can do the best job of crafting school improvement plans that use achievement data to spot problems and propose solutions.

According to *A National Study of Leadership in Middle Level Schools*, principals at 88% of U.S. middle schools report using leadership teams to advise them about decisions. Eighty-two percent of those teams include teacher representatives, 44% involve parents, 22% include community members, and 18% involve students.

However, the study noted, "Individuals other than the principals seldom made the decisions. . . . While principals described high levels of participation from almost all groups, in most cases that participation involved discussion rather than actual decision making." The study's authors expressed disappointment at the "low levels of collaboration," particularly when it has been shown to create the conditions for effective leadership and school improvement.

Traditionally, parents have played a fairly limited role in middle schools, focusing on tasks such as organizing fund-raisers, assisting in the cafeteria, and chaperoning field trips. Many parents acknowledge being perplexed about how to be involved in their children's middle schools, particularly when the youths express a desire for greater independence.

In recent years, with the push for public accountability of school performance, more parents have assumed leadership roles, including serving on committees that set school policies. Legislatures in many states have mandated that schools set up governance councils whose membership must include parent representatives. These councils perform a wide range of duties, such as hiring principals, setting discipline codes, and choosing the students' course of studies.

In some cases, these new governing groups haven't lived up to expectations, in part because of the huge investment of time and training that the volunteer positions require. In addition, administrators and teachers have not always appreciated what some believe is a movement to weaken their influence in public education.

Principals bear heavy responsibility, under state and federal accountability laws, for accelerating the learning of all students. However, local, state, and federal directives also can create conditions that make it difficult for principals to meet those goals. Parents should seek to understand and improve the conditions under which principals work wherever possible.

One of the principal's most important jobs, in collaboration with the school leadership team, is hiring and retaining effective staff members and releasing those who are incompetent or resist improvement. Gaining the authority to build an effective staff may sometimes require changes in contracts between the local teacher's union and the school district, especially seniority provisions.

School leaders also need significant authority over school resources. For example, teachers need flexibility in how they use class time so they can meet the needs of all students. Effective principals adjust the school schedule to provide this flexibility, and they make sure that teachers have time for professional learning that will improve their instruction.

In exchange for greater school autonomy, the school district must set high standards for performance. Parents can hold school leaders accountable for reaching them.

PUTTING PARENTS BACK IN SCHOOL

Although every parent can't be involved in the day-to-day operations of a middle school, all parents have the right and the responsibility to have an intimate connection with the schools their children attend. Studies indicate that most parents do not feel qualified to help make decisions about school governance or academic matters and prefer to perform such roles as restocking books in the school library or coordinating a bake sale. Yet experience also finds that parents can contribute to schools in substantial ways, given opportunity, encouragement, and training.

Consider how parents influence policy at O'Farrell Community School in San Diego. As a charter school serving about 1,500 mostly poor and minority students, O'Farrell was designed to be more responsive to parents than is typical for public schools in large urban districts. Living up to that ideal hasn't always been easy, however.

"It's a work in progress," acknowledges Byron King, chief education officer of the school.

He recalled that 10 years ago, when he was still a teacher at the school, the faculty debated whether to conduct meetings of the school's governing board at 2:30 P.M., which would suit most of the staff, or at 6:00 P.M., which would better accommodate parents' schedules. Opting for the later start time might seem a minor decision, he said, but it marked a "turning point" in the school's relationship with students' families because it signaled the staff's willingness to consider parents as an integral part of the school's operations.

"The level of rigor in the discussions inside the governing board increases tremendously when you have to answer to parents," King said. "They appreciate what we're doing but they push us. They want us to be clear. As educators, we promise a lot but we don't follow up on it. Parents are more likely to say to me, 'You said you were going to do this, we agreed on that, what's happened?' It increased our accountability for our operations."

Although the parents on O'Farrell's governing board have been extremely effective, they represent only a few of the families the school needs to reach. For assistance in motivating other parents to volunteer, O'Farrell turned to the Parent Alliance for School Standards (PASS), which worked closely with the school's development coordinator, Pat Vacio. Using a grant from the Edna McConnell Clark Foundation, O'Farrell hired three part-time parent liaisons who established personal relationships with the families of the school's lowest-achieving students. All of the parent liaisons had children at O'Farrell and came from the minority groups the school was targeting for special attention: Filipinos, Latinos, and African Americans.

By continually calling these families at home, breaking through their initial reluctance, and responding to their concerns, the parent liaisons were able to show them how to reinforce what the children were learning at school.

"We all know for sure that you can't" raise student achievement "until parents are up to the plate. And our parents don't know how to do it" because so many of them are immigrants who don't speak English or who have a very limited education, Vacio said. "A lot of us take it for granted, but all parents do not know how to be advocates for their children."

During the 2001–02 school year, Vacio persuaded teachers of the importance of conducting conferences with parents during the first month of school instead of waiting until after the children had failed a class. She also knew that parents of high- and average-achieving students wanted an opportunity to talk to teachers early in the year, too. Using the teachers' appointment books, Vacio, the parent liaisons, and some additional parent volunteers made thousands of phone calls on their behalf to set up the conferences. About 60% of O'Farrell's families eventually showed up to meet with their children's teachers.

The next year, after the school specified that teachers would not receive excellent ratings in their personnel evaluations unless they had met with most of their students' parents, Vacio and her team repeated their home contacts. This time they persuaded more than 80% of O'Farrell's families to attend the conferences. During the meetings, teachers and parents established personal learning goals for each student and discussed the school's larger objectives. The sessions proved so positive that 90% of the faculty asked for repeat sessions, and the number of parents who showed up for other school events during the school year tripled previous rates.

"It took a lot of pushing and pulling" to get many reluctant parents into the building, said Laura Juarez, one of the parent liaisons. "But once they came, they started coming and coming."

Juarez and the other liaisons provided a range of assistance to parents who had never before come to their children's schools. They found babysitters for parents who had no one to watch their youngsters, translated for those who didn't speak English, and explained their own struggles to understand school policies and practices. They also called the parents once a week to remind them to sign their children's daily planners, to ask about their homework, and to review their children's progress reports.

Besides improving the parents' relationships with O'Farrell's faculty and moving most of the targeted students off the school's failure list, the intervention process helped the parent liaisons develop their own leadership skills.

"You have no idea how much I learned," said Juarez, who emigrated from Mexico when she was a child. "I used to think, 'I can't ask that' [at a school meeting]. They'll think I'm stupid.'"

Working at O'Farrell and attending workshops sponsored by PASS showed her how to set higher standards for herself and her three school-age children.

"I'm pushing no bad grades in my family now," she said, "nothing lower than a C."

Byron King acknowledges that O'Farrell might not have established such positive relationships with families without the $20,000 foundation grant and the intervention of an outside group such as PASS. He believes that many middle school principals want to be more responsive to families but don't have staff members and volunteers with the time and the expertise to help.

"You have to spend some serious resources to get it to work," he said. "So a principal can work hard at it and be really concerned about it and not do the right things and get no payoff and then sort of give up. It's the same thing for teachers. Teachers understand on one level that it's important to involve parents, but most probably don't do a good job of that because they don't know how."

Groups such as PASS can help bridge the divide between school and home. Around the country, similar advocacy groups have sprung up to teach parents and educators how to work together for the benefit of all students. In Kentucky, for example, the Commonwealth Institute for Parent Leadership has trained hundreds of parents to advocate for improvements in public schools. Participants learn how to analyze school achievement data and work with the staff to design interventions that will help all students meet the state's standards.

"When I came, all I had was a desire to be a good volunteer," said parent Jennifer Buckman, but the Commonwealth Institute "gave me the knowledge and the confidence to get out and get things done and make a difference."

In 1991, parents from Jackson, Mississippi, who had persuaded more families to enroll their children in the local public schools, decided to expand their program nationally. Today the Parents for Public Schools organization has chapters in 15 states.

In Waco, Texas, Parents for Public Schools was concerned that many families were leaving for private schools when their children made the transition from the elementary to the middle grades. Believing that parents often acted because of misinformation, the group hosted a middle school fair to give families a chance to see what each public school had to offer (The district's open enrollment policy lets students choose any public school as long as there is space available). Educators discussed various program offerings, and students from each school took turns performing in jazz bands, orchestras, and theater productions.

"It proved to be empowering to parents of 4th- and 5th-grade students. They began to look at things differently," said Kris Olson, executive director of the Waco Parents for Public Schools chapter and communications director for the national group.

Through the national organization, Parents for Public Schools provides ongoing training and resources so participating parents can work with educators to improve instruction and learning. The group publishes newsletters on topics such as school leadership and produces a series of videotapes in English and Spanish, including explanations of academic standards, effective parent–teacher conferences, and an orientation to middle school.

"We are critical friends. We are part of identifying the issues and a part of solving them," Olson said. "It's to change the culture so that a school district cannot imagine not doing business without involving parents, rather than including parents as an afterthought."

AN INVITATION TO HELP

Although research indicates that most people are not involved in their community schools on a regular basis, they do have concerns about public education and believe that the success or failure of the schools has a huge impact on the community's well being. The majority of Americans are comfortable letting educators take charge of school policies unless the schools are not performing up to expectations.

Smart middle school principals don't wait for failure to ask for the public's help. They recognize that effective schools depend on assistance and expertise from a wide range of people, including teachers, parents, and students. They routinely issue invitations and provide support so that all groups feel connected to the school and capable of offering valuable leadership.

At Faubion Middle School in McKinney, Texas, principal Francisco Javier Oaxaca is using a grant from the MetLife Foundation Institute for Family Friendly Schools to reach out to the growing number of immigrant parents who have enrolled their children in recent years. By hiring a Spanish-speaking receptionist, recruiting bilingual tutors, translating school materials, training staff members to speak Spanish, and conducting parent meetings at convenient places throughout the community, Faubion has signaled a desire to partner with parents in helping their children succeed in school.

"We talk about it at every staff meeting, what are some things we can do," Oaxaca said.

The strategies certainly aren't unique to Faubion, he acknowledged, nor are they "earth-shattering" in their impact. But the gestures go a long way toward welcoming new families into the life of the school and showing respect for their contributions.

"Just having signs that say 'Welcome' in two different languages. They don't take a whole lot of time and energy," Oaxaca said. "It's not the big things that make you family-friendly. It's the little things you have to pay attention to."

Michael Graydoz takes that message to heart. As principal of Sunset Middle School in Longmont, Colorado, he understands implicitly that students' success stems from the collective force of many adults working on their behalf. His version of school leadership involves teams of people using their skills and energy to provide whatever students need.

"You have to include parents. You have to include community members. You have to have business partners to make it work. You can't do it yourself," he said. "I call it the triad—the parents, the community, the staff. They all have to meet to have a climate of learning. If you have one without the others, the triangle breaks down and you won't have relevant connections."

When Graydoz came to Sunset Middle School in 2000, he asked parents to hold coffees in their homes and invite neighbors so they could meet to discuss their concerns and expectations. These informal get-togethers laid the foundation for a series of initiatives that have helped the school revise the student handbook, improve test scores, encourage an increasing number of families to switch from private schools, and raise substantial sums of money for various projects.

When Sunset parents heard about a successful camping trip that a team of 7th grade teachers had sponsored to give students practical applications of history, math, and science lessons, they wanted every 7th grader to attend. Parents subsequently provided additional resources and planning so that by the following year all 7th graders could participate in the outdoors adventure.

A group of parents taught students how to design and produce an advertising brochure that Sunset could send to area businesses. Another parent who owns a printing company published the pamphlet at no cost to the school. Sunset subsequently attracted mentors and donations from more than a half-dozen major corporations in the area.

Parents also sponsored a fund-raising campaign when Sunset needed $4,000 to buy supplementary math materials for two groups of students—one group needing help bolstering basic skills and the other, accelerated learning. Recognizing that many families dislike traditional school fund-raising projects that expect children to sell selected products to relatives and friends, the parent organizers focused on obtaining direct cash donations. They advertised in the newspaper, draped banners over the school, and telephoned businesses and families at home. The payoff: about $12,000.

"Somebody knows somebody who can get us where we need to go," Graydoz said. "Parents have the local control, you empower them, they will do anything for you."

About 200 active volunteers work in the school throughout the year. They answer telephones in the office, staff a community reception area, direct after-school clubs, help grade research papers, and mentor struggling students. The regular presence of parents also lets teachers concentrate on improving instruction.

"As we are having to do more, better, faster, and are getting the professional training to do that, we have less time to coordinate spirit week or special events," said veteran language arts teacher Linda Bartlet. "If it weren't for our parents, inspiring kids beyond academics would not occur."

Danette Tye, whose oldest daughter, Katie, was an 8th grader at Sunset during the 2003–04 school year, said she appreciates the school's efforts to involve parents. When her daughter was in the 5th grade and the family was considering sending her to Sunset, Tye heard that parents weren't welcome at the school. She later shared that concern with teachers and administrators and worked with them to change the perception.

Admittedly, she said, parent involvement in the middle grades is not the same as she remembers from elementary school, where teachers and students embraced parents' efforts to help directly in the classroom. In middle school, parents might not always have direct physical contact with students, but they can continue being engaged by meeting and corresponding with teachers, assisting with tutoring and homework clubs, and monitoring homework and weekly progress reports.

"I send my children's teachers e-mails at the beginning of the year: 'Here are my child's strengths and weaknesses. I want to know immediately if there are problems,'" Tye said. "For instance, my oldest hates change. Even switching desks can be hard for her. So they try to work with her. If they don't know what to expect, they can't anticipate it."

Tye plans to intensify her school communications when her younger daughter enters Sunset. Because the child has epilepsy and learning disabilities, she will need plenty of guiding hands, Tye said.

One of her best role models might be her older sister, Katie, who recently discovered that middle school leadership is not just for adults. When Katie learned that one of her classmates wanted to buy an expensive prosthetic ear to cover a deformity, she enlisted her mother's help in coordinating a school fund-raising project. They sold raffle tickets, conducted an auction of donated memorabilia, and sponsored a walkathon, which they dubbed the "Buck-An-Ear Walk." Pledges and proceeds produced almost $10,000 for the boy's benefit.

In the process, Katie also taught her classmates how their ignorance and cruelty had nearly broken her friend's spirit.

"Sometimes I have social problems with others, them thinking I'm retarded or just not a normal person," Eduardo Montoya wrote in an essay included on the fund-raising flyers. "Throughout my life I've had several surgeries, especially on one ear. It was once a scar type thing then the surgeon tried to form it into an ear. On my other ear I have to use a hearing aid. When people look at that they mock me by yelling as if I cannot hear them."

By the end of the fund-raising campaign, Eduardo had attracted a flock of new friends and gained self-confidence talking to reporters, meeting with business sponsors, and sharing his story with students.

"He's always jumping around now," Katie told a reporter for the Boulder, Colorado *Daily Camera*. "His feet haven't touched the ground in three months."

For Katie's mother, the event symbolized the power of people combining their energy and talents to help children, which is the essence of an effective middle school. The event galvanized the school community, and teachers and administrators provided key support. Ultimately, however, the fund-raising project revealed that leadership is not defined by a person's age or position or power, but by his or her commitment to carry out a plan and rally others to the same cause.

"I can't tell you how many kids were handing out prizes, helping sell raffle tickets. They kind of took over the leadership of their little part, which was neat to see," Tye said. "It really brought the school together for a common goal."

As Sunset's experience shows, parents and students collectively can become a powerful force for change in middle schools. In the next chapter, we will look at specific ways in which parents individually can make a positive difference in their own children's lives.

"Get to Know Me Better!"

IF YOU LISTEN TO MEDIA COMMENTATORS, politicians, and many of your neighbors, you will get an earful of what's wrong with today's youth:

- They're loud.
- They're disrespectful.
- They listen to bad music.
- They dress weird.
- They are prone to violence.
- They watch too much television.
- They have no ambition.
- And they don't know as much about (FILL IN ANY SCHOOL SUBJECT) as previous generations did.

Perhaps those critics haven't heard about Jacob Komar, a 6th grader from Burlington, Connecticut, who refurbished 60 discarded computers and installed them in the homes of poor families in his community. Or Sasha Bowers, an 8th grader from Columbus, Ohio, who drew on her experience living in a homeless shelter to create a summer's worth of activities for 250 other displaced children in the area. Or Kristal DeRuisé, a 7th grader from Reno, Nevada, who raised $25,000 for Lupus research by painting and selling decorative rocks. These three adolescents were among 10 middle and high school students named America's top youth volunteers for 2003 by the Prudential Spirit of Community Awards.

Maybe those critics missed the stories about the three Native American middle-grades students from Minocqua, Wisconsin, who won a $25,000 Columbus Foundation Community Grant in 2002 to develop their idea of using weevils to eradicate the Eurasian Water Milfoil, a fast-growing weed that is choking lakes all over the country. Or the team of four middle-grades students from Brandon, Mississippi, who won first place in the 2002 Bayer/National Science Foundation Award for inventing the Stopping Cart, which incorporates handheld brakes on store carts to prevent them from crashing into cars and people.

Could be that those critics didn't know about the team from Lake Middle School in Denver, Colorado, that earned a spot in the 2002 National High School Cheerleading Competition in Orlando, Florida, but couldn't afford the $18,000 cost of the trip. Instead of pouting, the Lake Middle cheerleaders—who attend a school where 90% of the students are considered poor by federal standards—raised $4,000 to help another team from Denver go to the same competition.

"These are girls who have nothing other than their beautiful faces and their positive outlook," said Tiffany Bell, a 6th grade teacher at Lake Middle School. "These young women have obviously taught everyone a lesson."

Today's adolescents are no different from youngsters in other eras. Many of them are committed, capable, and civic-minded. They are passionate about contributing to their families and improving the society in which they were born. However, they also are prone to making mistakes, acting inappropriately, and following bad influences at times. That's why we refer to them as "growing up."

The strongest deterrent to poor choices is the consistent, positive guidance they receive from adults.

A 2002 survey of students ages 12 through 17 conducted by the nonprofit organization Communities in Schools found that teenagers who experience strong relationships with adults feel much safer and optimistic than those who do not. Young people with good support systems are more likely (58% versus 25%) to have never cheated on a test, to feel healthy (66% versus 5%), to feel happy (60% versus 37%), and to believe they will be successful in the future (84% versus 57%). In addition, when adults are strongly involved in their lives, students are nine times more likely to get straight A's in school.

Young people perform important leadership roles in about half the nonprofit organizations in the country. They are actively involved in politics, international relations, the environment, and social justice. Consider Aubyn Burnside, founder and CEO of Suitcases for Kids, which provides luggage to foster children so they aren't forced to carry their belongings in trash bags when they move. Aubyn, a North Carolina teenager who started Suitcases for Kids when she was 10, has overseen the charity's growth to all 50 states and 42 countries.

"This generation is just amazing in terms of its desire to give," said John A. Calhoun, president of the National Crime Prevention Council and founder of Youth as Resources, a program that recruits teenagers to design and carry out projects to solve problems in their neighborhoods. "They really believe they can and should make a difference."

Why, then, do such negative impressions of adolescents persist?

For one thing, many adults are quicker to criticize than to praise. Too often adults marginalize young people, neither soliciting nor welcoming their contributions. Adolescents, in turn, respond to being ignored either by misbehaving to gain attention or by disconnecting from those people who show little concern for them.

Poor perceptions of youths also thrive because the adults who could disprove the false impressions don't speak out on their behalf. Many adults lead busy lives, work long hours, and often forget to sing the praises of adolescents and thereby elevate their status in the community.

But more importantly, many adults don't really *know* today's adolescents. When they look at them, they don't see inside. They judge the quality and integrity of youths based on quick evaluations of their clothing, their music, or their quixotic behaviors.

Just one in 20 adults consistently relates to young people in a positive way, revealed "Grading Grown-Ups 2002," a recent national study conducted by the Lutheran Brotherhood and the Search Institute. The study found that while a strong majority of adults believes it's important to encourage success in school, teach shared values, guide decisionmaking, teach respect for cultural differences, and have meaningful conversations with adolescents, most do not follow through by acting on those beliefs.

"Kids need us, and we're letting them down," said Nathan Dungan, vice president of Lutheran Brotherhood, a financial services organization based in Minneapolis.

The two organizations offer many recommendations for adults who want to strengthen connections between the generations, including:

- Telling parents when their children do something responsible and generous
- Encouraging and participating in job shadowing and mentoring programs at the workplace
- Asking young people to work alongside you when volunteering
- Sharing values and beliefs with young people and asking them to share theirs

But the most important suggestion is a simple one—listen to them.

An 8th grader from Maine put it plainly in the surveys gathered for this book: "Talk about how I feel once in a while, not just how they feel."

A Minnesota 8th grader said she longs for the time when her parents would "just devote a whole day for us to be together. I just want them to be home more often so I can talk to them. So I don't feel lonely all the time."

BE INVOLVED IN THEIR LIVES

As we have stated repeatedly throughout this book, parents are the first and the strongest influence in an adolescent's life. A majority of the middle-grades students we surveyed praised their parents for raising them well, for caring about their education, for inspiring their intended careers, and for serving as positive role models in their increasingly turbulent world.

"My mom and dad love me *a lot*," a 7th grader from Vermont said about his parents.

A 6th grader from Kentucky said that in her family "we all work together. We're a never-ending chain."

And a 7th grader from New Mexico wrote this note to his parents at the end of his survey: "Thank you for taking care of me and feeding me and giving me shelter and someday I'm going to do something very special to you."

Yet, even when they are grateful for their parents' guidance and protection, many adolescents wish that their mothers and fathers would seek to know them better. While they don't expect or want them to wear the same clothes, watch the same MTV videos, or use the same expressions, adolescents wish their parents would consult and respect their opinions. A common theme among students at all grade levels was the desire for more genuine interest and attention from their parents—not just the regular pressure to get good grades in school.

> "Nobody understands me and then they yell at me and I cry," one 7th grader said.
>
> "Quit smoking!! Stop arguing! Set a good example for me!" said another.
>
> One 7th grader urged her parents to "spend more time with me, stop being so obsessed with work, don't give me supper at 9 o'clock, and know how to have fun!!!"
>
> "I'd say to lighten up and let me feel like I could talk to them," one 6th grader offered.
>
> "Teach me about drugs and how bad they are," another 6th grader pleaded.
>
> And one 6th grader offered this tongue-in-cheek cure for adolescent angst: "Let the kid have a dog and a really cool car and the kid will be an excellent child forever."

Over and over, students asked for more consideration from their parents. They want you to:

Quit comparing them to their siblings and friends.

"I try my best and you should appreciate *me*, not everyone else. I am me, and I need your support."

"Don't favor any one child!"

"If things are one way with one kid, it should be that way with all."

"I really think that they should tell me how proud they are of me more often. They mostly say it to my sister."

Be involved in their lives.

"Talk to me and find out more about what is going on at school."

"I wish I could have a loving and caring family because I need someone to love and care about me, besides boys."

"Talk to me more, especially my mom, and spend more time with me."

"Be a better parent. Pay attention to us. Take us out. Spend family time with each other. And never call us bad things."

Recognize their accomplishments, not just their faults.

"Don't lecture me every time I make a mistake for 10 minutes. Just remind me."

"Was I a good child?"

"They keep saying I'm going to fail."

"Be nice to me, let me have fun, treat me fairly and respectful."

"Encourage me."

Set reasonable, consistent limits for them.

"Don't be nice and let me be spoiled. Be overprotective."

"Do not let me stay up late on school nights."

"Be as hard as they can so I grow up right."

"Put restrictions on me, even though I might not like it now, I will thank you later."

"I don't need a friend. I need a parent."

Be firm, not punitive.

"You need to stop whipping me because that gets you nowhere. If you do whip me then I'm still gonna do what I've been doing."

"Tell kids to do something nicely, in soft tones."

"Don't yell at me, just talk to me when I get in trouble."

I would say to listen to my opinions and consider them before you say no. It might make both of us happier."

Pay attention to them but also respect their need for privacy.

"Sometimes I need space for myself."

"There are two other kids and two adults [in the family] and it gets crowded."

"Too much togetherness!"

"Don't worry about me so much! And please tell my sister not to read my e-mail over my shoulder!"

Don't assume the worst about them.

"I would tell them not to ground me some time. It's not my fault."

"Don't always do the talking. Let the child talk. Hear our side of the story!"

"I fight with my sister a lot and I always get in trouble when it's her fault."

Understand that they will need lots of practice before they learn how to behave appropriately in all situations.

"I can't do everything by myself so sometimes I need help."

"As hard as it may be, I need to make my own mistakes and learn from them."

"Give me time to think about life and it's not all gonna happen so quick. Give me some room to breathe."

"Their expectations for me are sometimes too high."

"Don't get mad at me because I am stupid."

Let them be more independent but keep an eye on them, too, so you can spot signs of trouble.

"Always make sure they know where I am."

"Watch me when I leave the house [and] get the number to the place I'm going to."

"Ask questions and always know what and where I'm going or doing."

"Talk to me about my friends! Please!"

Model the values you're teaching them.

"I wish they would follow the rules that they give me."

"Take me to church more."

"Do a good job. Be a parent."

One of the most important jobs parents have is caring about their children's education. You don't have to be president of the PTA, serve on school committees, or proctor study halls to gain credibility in your children's eyes. While schools always need volunteers for such positions, parents who can't fulfill conventional roles can still contribute in meaningful ways.

Do Your Parents Care About Your Education?

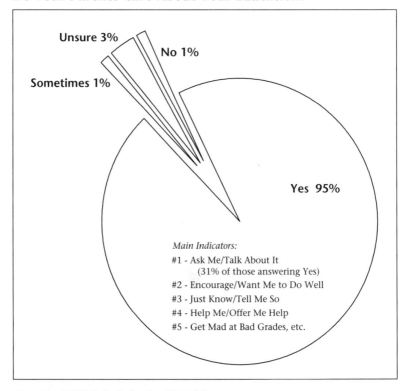

Unsure 3%

No 1%

Sometimes 1%

Yes 95%

Main Indicators:

#1 - Ask Me/Talk About It
    (31% of those answering Yes)
#2 - Encourage/Want Me to Do Well
#3 - Just Know/Tell Me So
#4 - Help Me/Offer Me Help
#5 - Get Mad at Bad Grades, etc.

In its 1999 study, *Playing Their Parts: Parents and Teachers Talk About Parental Involvement in Public Schools*, the nonpartisan research group Public Agenda found that 83% of parents believe the most vital role they can play is checking homework and encouraging their children to learn. Three-quarters of parents were so concerned about their child's education that they chose where they live in large part because of the quality of the local schools, and more than half (56%) said they interviewed the principal or teachers before they enrolled their children in those schools.

Most of the adolescents who completed our survey said they depend on their parents' strong presence in their lives, particularly with school. Ninety-five percent of the students said they know their parents are interested in their education because:

> "They look at my agenda and homework."
>
> "They come to everything that happens at school."
>
> "My mom is in college."
>
> ""They always ask what we're doing in my classes and look at my tests. They come to conferences and ask if I need help."
>
> "They encourage me and push me to do good. They are very supportive."
>
> "They meet with my teachers."
>
> "She makes me have good grades or I can't be on the Step team."
>
> "They talk about it every day."
>
> "She wants me to be somebody."
>
> "They're always asking me questions about things I learn."
>
> "I pretty much think that all parents are interested in their child's education. I know my parents are."

For all the good intentions, however, many parents acknowledge that they're not doing enough to help their children succeed in school. A demanding work schedule is a common excuse for doing less than their best, but many parents also feel inadequate to the task. They often don't understand their children's homework assignments and tests, they don't know where to draw the line between intervening and interfering, and they don't feel particularly welcome at school.

"What becomes quickly apparent from talking with parents is that whenever they have a dilemma or complicated decision to make, there is no one set strategy, no playbook, for them to rely on," Public Agenda noted in its 2002 report, *A Lot Easier Said Than Done: Parents Talk About Raising Children in Today's America*. "As a dad from Connecticut said, 'I want to know where the manual is. When you get a piece of electronics it [comes] with a book.' Instead, parents are struggling with many powerfully held—and sometimes contradictory—principles about raising children."

HOTLINE FOR HOMEWORK

Homework seems to be the universal hassle. Public Agenda's surveys indicate that at least half the parents in America have had a serious argument with their kids about homework. Yet most parents also consider homework valuable for their kids. According to an international poll taken in 1998, 78% of Americans believe homework is an essential school practice. In every other industrial nation surveyed, homework's approval ratings fell below 70%.

Although American parents generally support homework, they also wish it weren't so disruptive to their lives. Public pressure to reduce overwhelming amounts of out-of-school assignments has caused communities such as Piscataway, New Jersey, and Solana Beach, California, to place restrictions on homework in recent years.

Harris Cooper, a psychology professor at the University of Missouri-Columbia who is one of the nation's foremost experts on homework practices, acknowledges that while homework has a positive effect on achievement as children advance to the middle grades and beyond, the nightly assignments shouldn't be excessive. He recommends no more than 10 minutes per night per grade level, a formula with which groups such as the National PTA agree. At the recommended rate, an 8th grader could be expected to have up to an hour and 20 minutes of homework each night.

Homework Strategy (Best, Favorite, or Most Unusual)	
Just Do It/As Soon as Possible	35%
Get Organized/Use a Quiet Place/Take Breaks	17%
Prioritize (by Difficulty, Due Date, etc.)	11%
While Listening to TV/Music	10%
Other	10%
Make Sure I've Learned from It	9%
Work With a Classmate/Family Member	9%

Note: Due to rounding, totals do not equal 100%.

What should a concerned parent do to mitigate the homework hassles? First, remember that homework is only one part of the school equation. Although research indicates that poor homework practices often keep students from succeeding in school, few children manage to do homework well all the time. Plenty of students have gotten into Harvard and Yale without acing every homework assignment or, for that matter, remembering to turn in all of their assignments to their teachers. Perfection is an impossible goal. Don't make it yours.

Second, seek routines that fit your family. If the first hour after you arrive home from work is full of tense adjustments, don't schedule homework consultations then. It's a setup for disaster. Instead, give everyone time to get acclimated first. On the other hand, if afternoons are free at your house and you prefer to keep the evenings open for family activities, encourage your children to complete homework before supper. Devise a schedule that suits your style, and you will find it easier to stick to it.

Third, recognize that some homework assignments are boring. Life is full of such routine necessities—doing the laundry, shoveling the snow, and practicing for competitive athletic events, to name just a few. Children should understand that just as some mundane tasks help us maintain our households and our place on the team, others help us memorize multiplication tables so we can learn higher math.

At the same time, repetitive homework rarely motivates children to learn. Usually a teacher can tell if students understand how to convert ratios to fractions or identify the parts of speech based on their responses to five or six problems, so there's little point in asking them to complete 20 similar problems for homework. If your children routinely have excessive amounts of homework of this kind, ask their teachers for a lighter load. Make an appointment with the principal or the guidance counselor if the teachers balk without a reasonable explanation. Share some of your children's homework papers, which demonstrate mastery of the skills, to make the case for more appropriate assignments.

Finally, approach homework as a problem that can be solved. Investigate various options, try out different strategies, and settle on a few methods that seem promising, given your personal circumstances. Make adjustments later if necessary.

As a parent, you don't have to be a surrogate teacher. And you should never put yourself in the position of completing your children's homework for them. Instead, think of yourself as a conduit. You can provide encouragement and praise during difficult assignments. You can demonstrate the "homework" that adults have to complete, such as balancing a checkbook, paying household bills, and organizing volunteers for a civic function. You can find supplementary materials and activities that will give your children alternative ways to understand difficult material. But you don't have to sweat every algebra problem or stress every social studies project. You already put in your time at school, remember? Now it's your children's turn.

Here are some other key points about helping your children with homework:

- Your most important contribution might be showing your children how to organize their work. Teachers across the country identify disorderliness as the number one problem to staying on course with homework. Kathie Josephs, a middle school teacher and a tutor at an after-school homework center in Arizona, said she shows students how to separate their papers into color-coded notebooks and folders, how to clean out their backpacks once a week, and how to write down their homework assignments each day. "They get so far behind, they can't see the light," she said. "So you have to help them out of that hole. We help them set goals—sort of like getting out of debt. It just works. Some of the kids say, 'I've never been current before. I won't be grounded anymore.'" Chelsea, a 7th grader from Virginia, believes that "the best thing you can teach your child is time management. Those who learn how to handle a busy schedule, schoolwork, and a social life at a young age tend to do better academically."

- Make sure your children know how to find information, including using the dictionary, encyclopedias, and reference books. Plagiarism is on the rise in many schools because the Internet has made it so easy to insert documents and quotations directly into students' papers. Show your children how to properly cite someone else's work. Enlist a librarian's help if you are unsure about how to proceed.
- Don't be intimidated by homework in a subject you don't understand well or in which you struggled in school. Ask your children to explain the meaning of each part of a problem or assignment. Usually that explanation will give you enough information to find a solution. Encouraging children to explain their thinking also identifies gaps in their reasoning that might signal the need for additional review or different applications of the information that will help them understand it better.
- Organize a group of parents who will agree to serve as subject "experts" for the children in the group. If you're an engineer, you might volunteer to be the math homework consultant. A neighbor who's a whiz at computers might serve as the Internet research coach. Each of us has certain strengths that we can share, but we don't have to know everything to help our kids in school. Your best skill might be organizing the parent consultants and passing out the list of contacts and phone numbers.
- Create a checklist that you can run through every night with your children regarding homework. Some suggested questions: What is tonight's homework assignment? Do you understand how to do it? What is your study plan (for example, read the chapter and take notes, or write some review questions at the end and use that as the outline for a report)? If you have more than one assignment, how will you apportion your time? Do you need any special supplies, such as an encyclopedia or a poster board?
- If your children are having trouble with homework, consult their teachers to find out why. Do your children complete their assign-

ments but frequently turn them in past the deadline? Perhaps the
teachers could recommend some organizational strategies, such
as asking your children to write down each task in a notebook,
then check their accuracy with the teachers at the end of class.
One middle school student we know sends an e-mail message to
his teachers every three weeks and asks, "Am I okay? Am I miss-
ing any assignments?"

• Do the teachers frequently assign homework that requires supplies and resources you can't provide? If teachers understand
this, they can modify the assignment or make sure your children have access to supplies provided through the PTA or
school office.

• If your investigation of homework problems leads you to conclude that the teacher might be contributing to the tension,
don't go on the attack or make demands. Be polite and diplomat-
ic. Ask for help. Find some common ground, and always give the
teacher time to make adjustments. Prepare for a conference by
listing some of your concerns and observations, but understand
that your children's version of events might be somewhat
skewed. For example, your children might complain that their
homework was too easy, while teachers claim that your children's
assignments are so sloppy and incomplete that they assumed
they didn't understand the material. Sometimes acknowledging
inconsistencies can lead to better communications and help you
find long-term solutions. Suggest ways in which both of you can
make accommodations without losing sight of the objective—
helping your children succeed in school.

• Make sure your children receive regular feedback about homework. Not every assignment justifies detailed remarks, but children need specific suggestions about how they can improve and
areas in which they excelled. Such comments also affirm their
efforts and show them that homework matters. "I do not assign
anything I don't grade and put a comment on, and the students
know that," said Christy McNally, a 7th grade teacher from
Kansas. "Anything I assign, I look at and record. So the students
know they are doing something for a reason."

• If your child particularly enjoys certain kinds of homework—writing short stories using algebra terms, for example, or making a
board game incorporating Spanish grammar rules—send a note to
the teacher communicating your child's pleasure and encouraging the teacher to assign more homework of this type. Likewise,

you can ask your children's teachers if they periodically will let students create their own homework and test reviews. This will give your children some choice—which is one of the most effective ways to encourage learning—and play to their preferred learning style, at least part of the time. Most teachers have too many students to be able to customize homework assignments for each child. But teachers also struggle with homework compliance and usually will welcome suggestions from parents about how to help children reach their potential.

- Turn off the television set. Children in the United States watch an average of 3 to 5 hours of television daily. And it's not always educational fare. The average American adolescent sees more than 20,000 commercials a year. Why should you care about these statistics? Research has shown that the hours children spend watching television have a direct impact on their achievement in school. Break the habit now. When you turn off the tube, you will be amazed at how much time is left for learning, whether through homework, family conversations, or activities in which you participate together. Be a good role model for your child. Don't watch television yourself during the homework hour. In addition to eliminating another distraction from your child's study habits, you will send an important message by your actions. Children can see right through a double standard. To break the family's television habit, set a time limit for the week. Let your children review the television listings and prioritize the programs they will watch. If they use up their allotted time by Tuesday, they won't be able to watch anything else the remaining four days. Hold yourself to the same limits.
- Don't do your children's homework for them. By seemingly solving one problem, you create another. Teachers use homework to find out whether students understood the lesson or need additional help. Your answers won't tell them what they need to know. And when you overstep the boundaries by doing your children's homework for them, you send the message that you think they're not capable of doing it.
- Finally, let your children fail occasionally. If you try to rescue your children from every bad decision, such as driving to school to turn in the homework they left on the kitchen table, you will keep them from learning the consequences of their actions and the importance of being organized. Failure can be one of life's best teachers.

Adolescents learn best by direct experience. Jason, a 7th grader from Virginia, acknowledged that he used to "take forever" doing his homework. Distractions, difficult assignments, the siren song of pick-up basketball games—you name the excuse for procrastination, he had tried it.

Over time, he said, he experimented with different strategies, such as setting up an afternoon schedule, clearing the desk in his bedroom so he wouldn't be tempted to play instead of study, organizing his assignments in a binder every Monday, and starting on the hardest homework tasks first. Now he routinely makes the honor roll at his school, he qualified to take an algebra class for gifted students, and he gets his homework finished before 9:00 P.M. every evening.

"I find that a good night's rest leaves me fresh and ready to learn the next day," he said.

Ah, the wisdom of youth. Actually, adolescents do have some wise ideas about how to halt the homework hassles. Keep in mind that each child moves to a different beat. Work with yours to find a good rhythm.

"Maybe some people like to watch the clouds while doing homework. Others may like listening to trickling water," Jason said. "I experimented with things and found I liked working in a well-lit area. I like listening to music while I work. I put a plasma ball near my work area so I could look at the forever-changing patterns that the lights made while I worked."

Paying attention to your children's education matters. Parents who supervise homework, ask questions about their children's classes, meet with their teachers, provide quiet time to study, insist that their children take challenging courses, and encourage them to persist with difficult material set the foundation for lifelong learning and success.

But don't just take our word for it. Listen to your children.

❖ Appendix ❖

Survey Results:
What Matters to Kids
in the Middle

WE WANT TO THANK THE ADMINISTRATORS, TEACHERS, AND STUDENTS from all the schools that participated in the surveys collected for this book. We honored the principals' requests not to identify their schools or cities.

Thanks also to Patrick Barry, who designed the survey methodology and worked with Kelly Mazzoli and Thom Velez to tally and summarize the data.

During the 2002–03 school year, we sent the survey to middle school students and asked them about their favorite subjects, their most challenging assignments, and the level of safety in their schools, among other questions. A total of 2,369 6th, 7th, and 8th graders completed the survey. They attend public and private schools in Florida, Idaho, Kentucky, Maine, Massachusetts, Minnesota, New Mexico, and Vermont, representing a cross-section of the United States.

Because the schools had unequal numbers of students, we used a weighted distribution method to make sure their answers reflected the population at large. For example, private schools enroll 10% of American students, so answers from the two private schools in our survey each counted for 5% of the total results. We evaluated information from the eight public schools according to the geographic descriptions used by the U.S. Department of Education's National Center for Education Statistics. We placed each school within the appropriate geographic category, then weighted its statistics based on the likelihood of such a school being within the American public school system. For example, one in 10 U.S. schools is located in what's known as the "urban fringe" of cities with fewer than 400,000 people. So the survey responses from the school within the category of urban fringe accounted for 10% of the total results from public schools.

125

Size*	Type	Location**	Grades Taught	Surveyed
Small	Public	Suburban fringe of large city within MSA (population exceeding 400,000)	7–8	All
Small	Public	Rural town *not* within MSA (population less than 2,500)	6–8	All
Small	Public	Small town *not* within MSA (population of 2,500–25,000)	6–8	8
Medium	Private	Large central city of MSA (population exceeding 400,000)	K–12	6–8
Medium	Public	Rural town within MSA (population less than 2,500)	K–8	6–8
Medium	Public	Large urban town *not* within MSA (population exceeding 25,000)	7–8	All
Medium	Public	Suburban fringe of midsize city within MSA (population less than 400,000)	6–7	7
Medium	Public	Midsize central city of MSA (population less than 400,000)	6–8	All
Large	Private	Large central city of MSA (population exceeding 400,000)	K–12	6–8
Large	Public	Large central city of MSA (population exceeding 400,000)	6–8	6–7

* Small schools have an enrollment of less than 600 students in all grades taught; Medium schools have between 600 and 1,000; and Large have more than 1,000.

** The location of each school is identified here based on descriptions used by the U.S. Department of Education's National Center for Educational Statistics. MSA is a term used by the U.S. Census Bureau to describe a Metropolitan Statistical Area, i.e. a metropolitan-centered population that has statistically similar characteristics but may extend beyond its official political boundaries.

Students were inconsistent in answering all survey questions. The percentages reported here are based only on the number of students who responded to a given question. Percentages are rounded to the nearest 1%.

Although this study includes a representative sampling of students, it would be imprudent to assume that every conclusion applies to every middle school.

We included the results of most survey questions throughout the book. The tables and charts, which are included below and in other chapters, list the students' answers in order, from the most commonly mentioned to the least frequent. Where girls' and boys' answers were consistent, only the combined percentages are provided. Where there were notable differences between the two genders, we compared the results.

Permission to reprint any of the tables and charts included in this book must be obtained in writing from the copyright holders, Holly Holland and Patrick Barry. Please address correspondence to 4004 Alton Road, Louisville, KY 40207-4524 or to hollyholland@mindspring.com.

Students' Perspectives Concerning School	Girls	Boys
I am working as hard as I can in school.	67%	61%
My teachers know me well and challenge me to do my best.	58%	52%
I would work a lot harder if my classes were more interesting.	47%	52%
I usually look forward to going to school.	49%	40%
Most of my assignments have no connection to the real world.	18%	25%
My teachers are too demanding. I can't handle the pressure.	17%	20%
My teachers don't expect much of me, so I do just enough to get by.	12%	16%
I misbehave when I don't know an answer or didn't study for a test.	7%	11%

Note: Because some respondents chose more than one response, totals do not equal 100%.

Career Interests	Girls	Boys
Professional Sports	4%	27%
Health Care	20%	10%
Other	9%	12%
Science/Engineering/Computers	4%	16%
Entertainment	14%	5%
Law	11%	7%
Art/Design	11%	4%
Public Safety/Military Service	2%	11%
Publishing/Communications/Business	8%	4%
Veterinary Medicine/Animal Care	7%	4%
Education	9%	1%

Note: Due to rounding, totals do not equal 100%.

Biggest Fear	Girls	Boys
Classic Phobia (heights, the dark, etc.)	19%	17%
Animals/Bugs	23%	7%
Nothing	5%	24%
Anger/Authority	11%	15%
Death/Dying	13%	11%
Crime	11%	12%
Other	8%	10%
Abandonment/Being Alone	10%	3%

Note: Due to rounding, totals do not equal 100%.

Most Effective Way to Study for Tests	Girls	Boys
Have Family/Friend Study With/Quiz Me	27%	16%
Review Notes/Related Material	9%	17%
Memorization/Self-Quizzing	10%	16%
Study a Little Bit Daily/In Advance	11%	11%
Read and Reread	12%	10%
Other	8%	12%
Use Mnemonics/Games/Flash Cards	12%	5%
Cram/Procrastinate	4%	8%
Find a Quiet Place	4%	4%
While Listening to TV/Music	4%	0%

Note: Due to rounding, totals do not equal 100%.

Is There at Least One Adult in Your School Who Cares About You and Helps You Solve Problems?	
Yes	84%
No	15%
Maybe/Unsure	1%

Do You Have Some Good Friends at Your School?	
Yes	95%
No	4%
Maybe/Unsure	1%

Resources for Parents

The **U.S. Department of Education's** website (www.ed.gov) has many resources for parents, including topics covered on its monthly television series, free and inexpensive publications, and a searchable database on nearly every education topic. For more information about The Partnership for Family Involvement in Education, call toll free 800-USA-LEARN. Or, to locate your state Parent Information and Resource Center, call toll free 888-385-7222.

National Middle School Association (NMSA) recently updated *This We Believe: Successful Schools for Young Adolescents*, a guide to developing academically rigorous and developmentally responsive middle-level schools based on 14 key characteristics. Appropriate for both parents and educators, *This We Believe* includes a new section that fully describes the characteristics of young adolescents for parents. The 64-page book costs $8 ($6.40 plus shipping for NMSA members). Another useful resource from NMSA is *H.E.L.P. How to Enjoy Living with a Pre-Adolescent*, available in both English and Spanish. A packet of 50 brochures costs $22 ($17.50 for NMSA members). To order either of the publications, call 800-528-6672, or go to NMSA's online bookstore at www.nmsa.org.

The **Center for School, Family and Community Partnerships at Johns Hopkins University** (www.csos.jhu.edu) conducts research and analyzes policies to help parents, educators, and other community members work together to improve schools and boost student achievement. The center has collected a wide range of resources about home-school collaborations. Reprints of articles, handbooks, questionnaires, and program materials are available at a nominal cost.

At the website operated by the **National Forum to Accelerate Middle-Grades Reform** (www.mgforum.org), you can find information about national and regional change initiatives as well as other useful research and resources. Check out the "Just for Families and Students" section.

Improving the Odds: The Untapped Power of Schools to Improve the Health of Teens and *Promoting Student Connectedness to School: Evidence from the National Longitudinal Study of Adolescent Health* are two reports prepared by researchers at the Center for Adolescent Health at the University of Minnesota. The reports, which are based on findings from the largest survey ever conducted with adolescents in the United States, conclude that students who get along well with their teachers and fellow classmates and who feel cared for at school are at lower risk of violence, substance abuse, suicide, and pregnancy. The first report is available online at http://allaboutkids.umn.edu/kdwbvfc/fr_pub.htm or from the Center for Adolescent Health, University of Minnesota, 200 Oak Street SE, Suite 260, Minneapolis, MN 55455-2002. For information, e-mail: aph@umn.edu. The second report was published in the April 2002 issue of the *Journal of School Health.*

The **National PTA** publishes *A Compact for Learning: An Action Handbook for Family-School-Community Partnerships.* Other resources are available, many in Spanish. Go to www.pta.org/parentinvolvement.

The **Edna McConnell Clark Foundation** was one of the early advocates and sponsors of middle-grades education reform in U.S. schools. Many of the foundation's reports are available free through its website. Go to www.emcf.org and click on the Program for Student Achievement.

The **National Bullying Awareness Campaign**, a project of the National Education Association, seeks to reduce and eventually eliminate bullying in the nation's public schools. The campaign's website (www.nea.org/issues/safescho/bullying.html) includes information about the parent's role in preventing bullying and tips on what to do when a child is being bullied.

Parent Leadership Associates (PLA), a collaboration between the Prichard Committee for Academic Excellence and KSA-Plus Communications, offers several free guides and reports to help parents advocate for their children and work more effectively with their schools. The resources include an online quiz to see whether your child attends a "welcoming school" and "12 Things You Should Know and Expect from Your Schools . . . and Yourself." You can download the tools at PLA's website, www.plassociates.org. For information about the Commonwealth Institute for Parent Leadership, go to www.cipl.org.

The **Partnership for Learning**, a national nonprofit organization that helps schools and communities work together, has a large assortment of middle-grades resources on its website, including articles, books, and online links. An interesting feature is the "Must Have Skills" for each grade level. Go to www.partnershipforlearning.org.

The **National Association for the Education of African American Children with Learning Disabilities** offers a free handbook for parents. You can download the guide at www.charityadvantage.com or contact the association at 614-237-6021 or email info@aacld.org.

Parents for Public Schools, a national advocacy organization with local chapters in 14 states, offers a variety of free and inexpensive resources through its website—www.parents4publicschools.com—and a toll-free telephone number, 800-880-1222.

The **Afterschool Alliance** is a nonprofit organization dedicated to raising awareness of the importance of after-school programs and advocating for quality, affordable programs for all children. A guide for parents and others interested in starting after-school programs can be found at www.afterschoolalliance.org/start_a_program.cfm.

A Community Action Guide to Teacher Quality, published in 2002 by the Public Education Network, is designed to help parents and other community members assess teacher quality, identify ways to improve instruction, and put those strategies into place. The guide is available free from the Public Education Network, 601 Thirteenth Street NW, Suite 900 North, Washington, DC 20005, 202-628-7460 or at www.PublicEducation.org.

Notes

Introduction

Page vii: "He sleeps with stuffed animals": Holly Holland, "Editor's Note," *Middle Ground*, National Middle School Association, April 2002, Vol. 5, No. 5, p. 2.

Chapter 1

Page 5: "One group of 6th graders decided to teach citizenship skills": *Corporation for National and Community Service, Students in Service to America: A Guidebook for Engaging America's Students in a Lifelong Habit of Service,* Washington, DC, 2002, pp. 16–17.

Page 11: "One out of every six American children": Children's Defense Fund, *The State of America's Children Yearbook 2001,* http://www.childrens-defense.org/release010417.html.

Page 11: "more poor children live in suburban and rural areas": Alliance for Excellent Education, "Straight A's: An Update on Public Education: Policy and Progress," Vol. 2, No. 22, Dec. 9, 2002, p. 2.

Page 12: "In its 2001 survey of 40,000 middle and high school students": Catherine Gewertz, "No Racial Gap Seen in Students' School Outlook," *Education Week,* Nov. 20, 2002, Vol. 22, No. 12, p. 5.

Page 12: "Kids come to us with different degrees of confidence": Ibid.

Page 13: "However, such study should not be limited to 'heroes and holidays'": J. A. Banks. (1995). Multicultural education and the modification of students' racial attitudes. In W. D. Hawley & A. W. Jackson (Eds.), *Toward a Common Destiny: Improving Race and Ethnic Relations in America* (p. 331). San Francisco: Jossey-Bass.

Page 14: "In many American communities": Mary Pipher, *The Middle of Everywhere: The World's Refugees Come to Our Town,* Harcourt, Inc., New York, 2002, p. 13.

Page 14: "In a 1998 survey of young teens": KidsPeace, *1998 National Early-teen Survey: A Report to Congress and the Nation,* Sept. 23, 1998, Orefield, PA, 800-25-PEACE.

Page 15: "reports UCLA researcher Norweeta Milburn": Milburn, N. G., Rotheram-Borus, M. J., May, S., Rice, E., Brumback, B., Mallett, S. M., Rosenthal,

D., Zhou, K., & Witkin, A. "Adolescents exiting homelessness." In M. J. Rotheram-Borus (Chair), *Trajectories of homeless adolescents: Experiences while homeless and paths out of homelessness.* Symposium conducted at the 70th annual meeting of the Society for Research in Child Development, Tampa, FL.

Page 15: "According to the University of Michigan's 1997 nationally representative sample": The University of Michigan News and Information Services at http://www.umich.edu/~newsinfo/Releases/2001/May01/r05090 1a.html, http://umich.edu/~newsinfo/Releases/1998/Nov98/r110998a.html, and http://www.psc.isr.umich.edu/pubs/papers/rr01475.pdf.

Page 16: "As Hayes Mizell": "What Parents Need to Know About Middle School Reform," remarks of M. Hayes Mizell on October 16, 2002, at a public lecture in Nyack, New York. The lecture was sponsored by Nyack Partners in Education; the Nyack branch of the National Association for the Advancement of Colored People; Head Start of Rockland; the Rockland 21st Century Collaborative for Children and Youth; Brenda Ross; and the Nyack schools.

Page 18: "Suttons Bay, Michigan": Judy Rosenfield, "Surfing the Brainwaves: Making Sense of New Research About Habits of the Mind," *Middle Ground*, National Middle School Association, Columbus, Ohio, Vol. 5, No. 5, April 2002, p. 13.

Page 18: "Much of what we remember": Rick Wormeli, *Meet Me in the Middle: Becoming an Accomplished Middle-Level Teacher*, Stenhouse Publishers, Portland, Maine, p. 20.

Page 19: "The brain is a snowflake": Judy Rosenfield, "Surfing the Brainwaves," *Middle Ground*, p. 16.

Page. 19: "Lisa": Rick Wormeli, *Meet Me in the Middle*, p. 71.

Page 22: "Such achievement": Anthony W. Jackson and Gayle A. Davis, *Turning Points 2000: Educating Adolescents in the 21st Century*, Teachers College Press, New York, 2000, pp. 8–9.

Page 23: "School is not a bad place": *The Metlife Survey of The American Teacher 2001: Key Elements of Quality Schools*, MetLife, Inc., New York, p. 44, see *www.metlife.com.*

Page 23: "Some educators believe that groups of students are less able to achieve": *Turning Points 2000*, pp. 11–13.

Page 23: "According to 'Monitoring the Future'": Siobhan McDonough, "Survey: Teen Drug Use Declining," Associated Press and *The Courier-Journal*, Louisville, Kentucky, Dec. 17, 2001, p. A11.

Page 24: "According to national studies, 14–20% of girls and 20–22% of boys": 14 and Younger: The Sexual Behavior of Young Adolescents (Summary), *The National Campaign to Prevent Teen Pregnancy*, 2003, pp. 5-6.

Page 24: "And every year about three million teenagers": *Turning Points 2000*, p. 7.

Page 24: "Surveys from the 2000 National Longitudinal Study": Jessica Portner, "Teens' Risky Behavior Tied to School Troubles," *Education Week*, Editorial Projects in Education, Washington, DC, Vol. 20, No. 14, p. 5. See also "Feeling Connected to School Is Key to Adolescent Health," *American School Board Journal*, June 2002, pp. 6–8.

Chapter 2

Page 28: "6th, 7th, and 8th grades sometimes were appended to elementary schools": Paul S. George and Kathy Shewey, *New Evidence for the Middle School*, National Middle School Association, 1994, p. 4.

Page 29: "By the turn of the 21st century": Fredreka Schouten, "Kids like get-out-of-junior high card," Gannett News Service, Oct. 16, 2002, www.middleweb.com/MGNEWS1/MGN1019.html

Page 29: "In a 1996 study": Kenneth McEwin, Thomas S. Dickinson, and Doris M. Jenkins, *America's Middle Schools: Practices and Progress-A 25-Year Perspective*, National Middle School Association, 1996, p. 61.

Page 30: "Hayes Mizell": M. Hayes Mizell, *Shooting for the Sun: The Message of Middle School Reform*, The Edna McConnell Clark Foundation, 2002, pp. 37–41.

Page 30: "school board members and superintendents often do not understand the special needs of young adolescents": Ibid.

Page 30: "William Schmidt": Fredreka Schouten, "Kids like get-out-of-junior high card," Gannett News Service, Oct. 16, 2002, www.middleweb.com/MGNEWS1/MGN1019.html

Page 31: "Yet research shows that parents become much less involved": Jodie Morse, "When Parents Drop Out," *Time*, May 21, 2001, Vol. 157, No. 20, pp. 80–83.

Page 31: "Turning Points 2000 design includes seven key recommendations": *Turning Points 2000*, p. 27.

Page 32: "Turning Points 2000 calls for middle schools": Ibid., pp. 23–25.

Page 33: "Barren County": Terri West and Joan Lipsitz, "Schools to Watch: Middle Grades Reform Project Recognizes Success," *Middle Ground*, National Middle School Association, February 2000, Vol. 3, No. 4, p. 26.

Page 34: "Compton-Drew Investigative Learning Center (ILC) Middle School": Catherine Cobb Morocco et al., "Cultures of Excellence and Belonging in Urban Middle Schools," *RMLE Online*, National Middle School Association, April 2002, Vol. 25, No. 2, pp. 7–8.

Page 35: "George Fox Middle School": "Opening Doors to the Future: Preparing Low-Achieving Middle Grades students to Succeed in High School," *2002 Outstanding Practices*, Southern Regional Education Board, Atlanta, Georgia, pp. 9–12.

Page 37: "Many parents are so stressed": Hayes Mizell, "What Parents Need to Know About Middle School Reform," pp. 10, 15.

Page 39: "Education researchers Olga Reyes and Karen Gillock": Susan Black, "The Next Step: Major School Transitions Require More than a One-Shot Orientation," *American School Board Journal*, November 1999, Vol. 87, No. 11, p. 55.

Page 39: "In a 1996 study": Ibid.

Page 40: "By contrast, middle and high schools": Nancy Mizelle and Judith L. Irvin, "What Research Says: Transition from Middle School into High School," *Middle School Journal*, National Middle School Association, May 2000, p. 58.

Page 40: "high school students indicated that if their middle school teachers":"Helping Middle School Students Make the Transition Into High School," a digest prepared by ERIC Clearinghouse on Elementary and Early Childhood Education, Champaign, Illinois, www.kidsource.com/education/middlehigh.html.

Page 40: "The importance of parents being involved:" Ibid.

Page 41: "What matters most": Steve Farkas et al., *Playing Their Parts: Parents and Teachers Talk About Parental Involvement in Public Schools*, Public Agenda, 1999, New York, p. 35.

Page 41: "As a Texas teacher said": Ibid., p. 22.

Page 41: "Deborah Bova": MiddleWeb Listserv Conversation, "A Million Words: A Wonderful Tool to Connect with Parents." Retrieved February 7, 2003 from MiddleWeb site: http://www.middleweb.com/MWLISTCONT/MSL millionwords.html.

Chapter 3

Page 44: "If we have teachers who can 'teach them all'": Every Child Counts: Jefferson County Community Accountability Team, *Raising Student Achievement in the Middle Grades*, a report sponsored by the Prichard Committee for Academic Excellence and the Edna McConnell Clark Foundation, 2001.

Page 44: "Although teachers can't create individual lessons for every student": Ideas and phrasing for this section taken from Holly Holland, "Reaching All Learners," *Middle Ground*, National Middle School Association, April 2000, Vol. 3, No. 5, pp. 10–11.

Page 45: "With differentiation, teachers sometimes will vary the *content*": University of Virginia education professor Carol Ann Tomlinson is credited with the explanation of the breakdown of differentiation into content, process, and product; multiple sources.

Page 45: "Kari Sue Wehrmann": material based on direct interviews and information from Kari Sue Wehrman, "Baby Steps: A Beginner's Guide," *Educational Leadership*, September 2000, Vol. 58, No. 1, www.ascd.org/reading-room/ edlead/0009/wehrmann.html

Page 50: "In a recent study of 100,000 middle and high school students": Julie Blair, "Study Says School Atmosphere Fosters Abuse of 'Nerds,'" *Education Week*, Feb. 19, 2003, Vol. 22, No. 23, p. 10.

Page 51: "In one study of urban, suburban, and rural middle schools": Gerald K. LeTendre, Ph.D., "Downplaying Choice: Institutionalized Emotional Norms in U.S. Middle Schools," paper presented at the American Sociological Association meeting in Washington, DC, Aug. 12–15, 2000.

Page 52: In reality, tracking students into classes by 'ability' is not a neutral, objective process. As several researchers have pointed out, poor, minority, and immigrant children are over-represented in the low-level classes." J. H. Braddock. (1989). *Tracking of Black, Hispanic, Asian, Native American, and White Students: National Patterns and Trends*. Baltimore, MD: Center for Research on Effective Schooling for Disadvantaged Students. J. Oakes. (1995). More than meets the eye: Links between tracking and the culture of schools. In H. Pool & J. A. Page (Eds.), *Beyond tracking: Finding success in inclusive schools* (pp. 59–68). Bloomington, IN: Phi Delta Kappan Educational Foundation. J. Oakes, A. Gamoran, & R. N. Page. (1992). Curriculum differentiation: Opportunities, outcomes, and meanings. In P. W. Jackson (Ed.), *Handbook of Research on Curriculum* (pp. 570–608). New York: Macmillan.

Page 52: "Tracking also reinforces the 'bell curve view' of human intelligence that considers intelligence fixed": J. D. Bransford, A. L. Brown, & R. R. Cocking. (Eds.). (1999). *How People Learn: Brain, Mind, Experience, and School*. Washington, DC: National Academy Press.

Page 52: "Jefferson County (Louisville, Kentucky) Schools": Description part of an unpublished report written by Holly Holland and prepared for the Prichard Committee for Academic Excellence, funded by the Edna McConnell Clark Foundation, 2002.

Page 54: "every state but Iowa to adopt content standards in most subjects and grade levels": Joseph J. Pedulla et al., "Perceived Effects of State-Mandated Testing Programs on Teaching and Learning: Findings from a National Survey of Teachers," National Board on Educational Testing and Public Policy, Boston College, March 2003, p. 10.

Page 54: "the majority of teachers believe that state testing programs have had a negative effect on their instruction": Ibid., pp. 3–4.

Page 56: "At Broad Meadows Middle School": Ron Adams, "Writing Wrongs . . . Business Letters Give Students a Voice in World Affairs," *Middle Ground*, National Middle School Association, August 2001, Vol. 5, No. 1, pp. 36–37.

Page 57: "Teachers should check for understanding all along the way, not just by testing students at the end of each unit. And they should use a variety of assessment methods that give students multiple means of showing what they have learned. In addition to quizzes and tests, teachers can use interviews, questionnaires, conferences, class discussions, informal observations of small groups, and projects": *Turning Points 2000*, p. 55.

Page 57: "With each assessment, whether formal or informal, teachers are looking for evidence of learning.: *Turning Points 2000*, p. 56.

Page 57: "Grant Wiggins and Jay McTighe argue that teachers should think of students 'like juries think of the accused'": G. Wiggins, & J. McTighe (1998). *Understanding by Design*. Alexandria, VA: Association for Supervision and Curriculum Development.

Page 57: "Dr. Keen Babbage": Material based on direct interviews and information from Keen J. Babbage. (2002). *Extreme Teaching*, The Scarecrow Press, Inc., Lanham, Maryland.

Chapter 4

Page 61: "Research overwhelmingly supports": Peter C. Scales, "Care & Challenge: The Sources of Student Success," *Middle Ground*, National Middle School Association, October 1999, Vol. 3, No. 2, p. 21.

Page 62: "But Laurence Steinberg": Lynn Olson, "Detachment Starts in Middle School, Study Finds," *Education Week*, May 29, 2002, Vol. 21, No. 38, p. 9.

Page 63: "strong social relationships among students": Robert William Blum, Clea McNeely, and Peggy Mann Rinehart, "Improving the Odds: The Untapped Power of Schools to Improve the Health of Teens," Center for Adolescent Health and Development, University of Minnesota, 2002, p. 13.

Page 63: "Blum also confirmed": Ibid., p. 16.

Page 64: "Researchers studying the Chicago Public Schools": David T. Gordon, "Fuel for Reform: The Importance of Trust in Changing Schools," *Harvard Education Letter*, July/August 2002, Vol. 18, No. 4, pp. 1–4.

Page 66: "At University Park Campus School": Elizabeth Armstrong, "The Principal Who Knows Their Names," *The Christian Science Monitor*, April 1, 2003, www.csmonitor.com/2003/0401/p21s01-lecs.html.

Page 67: "Blum, the researcher": Michael A. Fletcher, "Connectedness Called Key to Student Behavior," *Washington Post*, April 12, 2002, p. A3.

Page 67: "Small enough so that people can know one another": Mary Anne Raywid and Libby Oshiyama, "Musings in the Wake of Columbine," *Phi Delta Kappan*, Vol. 81, No. 6, p. 446.

Page 68: "Consider Ditmas School": *Turning Points 2000*, pp. 126–127.

Page 69: "Researchers have found that teachers and students": Ibid., p. 129.

Page 69: "Researcher Linda Darling-Hammond observes that": L. Darling-Hammond (1997). *The Right to Learn: A Blueprint for Creating Schools That Work*. San Francisco: Jossey-Bass, p. 167.

Page 70: "Sidwell Friends Middle School": Jen Cort, "Good Advice: Regular Remodeling Reinforces the Foundation of School Advisory Programs," *Middle Ground*, National Middle School Association, October 1999, Vol. 3, No. 2, pp. 44–45.

Chapter 5

Page 75: "That's why parents 'with the time and skills to do so work very hard'": Kati Haycock, "Good Teaching Matters . . . A Lot," *Thinking K–16*, The Education Trust, Vol. 3, No. 2, Summer 1998, p. 3.

Page 76: "When asked to rate the importance of several school reform measures, 9 out of 10 parents in a 1998 national public opinion poll": Jeff Archer, "Public Prefers Competent Teachers to Other Reforms, Survey Finds," *Education Week*, November 25, 1998, Vol. 18, No. 13, p. 6.

Page 76: "Sanders tracked the progress of about 17,000 other students": David Hill, "He's Got Your Number," *Teacher Magazine*, May/June 2000, pp. 43–44.

Page 77: "the profession does not attract the best students": *Meeting the Highly Qualified Teachers Challenge: The Secretary's Annual Report on Teacher Quality*. Washington, DC: U.S. Department of Education, 2002, p. 12.

Page 77: "Almost one-third of new teachers": Vivian Troen & Katherine C. Boles, *Who's Teaching Your Children?* Yale University Press, New Haven, Connecticut, 2003, p. 16.

Page 77: "Schools of education": *Meeting the Highly Qualified Teachers Challenge*, p. 13.

Page 77: "schools in impoverished areas have the highest percentages": R. M. Ingersoll, "The Problem of Underqualified Teachers in American Secondary Schools," *Educational Researcher*, March, 1999, Vol. 28, No. 2, p. 29.

Page 78: "Yet only 51% of teacher education programs include any courses on middle-level teaching": *Turning Points*, p. 98.

Page 78: "and only 23 states currently offer middle-level certification": Catherine Gewertz, "Qualifications of Teachers Falling Short," *Education Week*, June 12, 2002, Vol. 21, No. 40, pp. 1, 18.

Page 80: "One study estimated that teacher turnover": "The Cost of Teacher Turnover," *Research Brief*, Association for Supervision and Curriculum Development, April 15, 2003, Vol. 1, No. 8, www.ascd.org/publications/ researchbrief/volume1/v1n8.html.

Page 81: "Whatever form professional development takes": J. Renyi (1996). *Teachers take charge of their learning: Transforming professional development for student success.* Washington, DC: National Foundation for the Improvement of Education.

Page 82: "And, as described in *Turning Points 2000*, 'a study of more than a thousand school districts concluded that every additional dollar spent on highly qualified teachers netted greater improvements in student achievement than did any other use of school resources'": *Turning Points 2000*, p. 116. R. Ferguson (1991, Summer). Paying for public education: New evidence on how and why money matters. *Harvard Journal on Legislation*, 28, 465–498.

Chapter 6

Page 86: "According to researcher": Eric Jansen, *Teaching with the Brain in Mind, Association for Curriculum Development*, Alexandria, Virginia, 1998.

Page 87: "According to the Justice": Kim Brooks, Vincent Schiraldi, and Jason Ziedenberg, "School House Hype: Two Years Later," a 1999 report of the Justice Police Institute/Children's Law Center. http://www.cjcj.org/schoolhousehype/ sh2.html#reality.

Page 87: "U.S. Census Bureau": *1998 Statistical Abstract*, Washington, DC, U.S. Census Bureau.

Page 87: "Specifically, data released by the": *Indicators of School Crime & Safety*, Washington, DC, National Center for Education Statistics, 2000.

Page 88: "In a national poll": www.discovery.com/stories/history/hateviolence/hateviolence.html.

Page 88: "And 14%": "Facing the Hard Facts in Education Reform," Educational Testing Service, Princeton, New Jersey, July 2001, p. 10.

Page 90: "Students in 5th": *Youth and Violence: Colorado Students Speak Out for a More Civil Society*, The Colorado Trust and the Families and Work Institute, 2002, www.coloradotrust.org.

Page 90: "While crimes on school campuses decreased": National Center for Education Statistics and Bureau of Justice Statistics, *Indicators of School Crime and Safety 2002*, U.S. Department of Education, Office of Educational Research and Improvement, NCES 2003-009, U.S. Department of Justice, Office of Justice Programs, NCJ 196753, November 2002.

Page 90: "Researchers have found that school bullying affects one third of middle-grades students": Nansel, T. R., Overpeck, M., Pilla, R. S., Ruan, W. J., Simons-Morton, B. & Scheidt, P. "Bullying behaviors among US youth:

Prevalence and association with psychosocial adjustment," *JAMA*, April 25, 2001, Vol. 285, No. 16, pp. 2094–2100.

Page 91: "In early 2003: results of a survey by Wirthlin Worldwide for the National Crime Prevention Council, 2003. www.center-school/viol_prev/css/ncpc1-16-03.pdf.

Page 91: "In their 1998 study of adolescent health": Blum, R. W., McNeely, C. A., Rinehart, P. M. (2002). *Improving the odds: The untapped power of schools to improve the health of teens*. Center for Adolescent Health and Development, University of Minnesota, Minneapolis, MN.

Page 94: "About 15 million children": News release, After School Alliance, Washington, DC, October 30, 2002, www.afterschoolalliance.org.

Page 95: "Educational researcher": Reginald M. Clark, "Why Disadvantaged Students Succeed: What Happens Outside School Is Critical," *Public Welfare*, Spring 1990, pp. 17–23.

Page 95: "Public support for after-school programs is strong, with 94% of those surveyed saying they want after-school programs and are willing to use federal and state funds to pay for them": "Afterschool Alert Poll Report," conducted by the Afterschool Alliance, Washington, D.C., July–August 2001.

Page 96: "Consider the results of": "The Annual State of Our Nation's Youth Report," the Horatio Alger Association, 2003. www.horatioalger.com.

Chapter 7

Page 97: "I have come to believe that the principal is the most instrumental person in education": *Parent Press*, the newsletter of Parents for Public Schools, Jackson, Mississippi, December 2000, p. 3.

Page 98: "Up until now, involvement of parents": Andreae Downs, "It's All in the Family: Middle Schools Share the Secrets of Parent Engagement," *Middle Ground*, National Middle School Association, February 2001, Vol. 4, No. 3, p. 11.

Page 98: "Research has demonstrated that democratically run schools are more effective": *Turning Points*, pp. 146–147.

Page 98: "Studies of leadership in schools with high student achievement": *Monitoring School Quality: An Indicators Report*, National Center for Education Statistics, Washington, DC, U.S. Department of Education, NCES 2001-030, December 2000, pp. 38–39.

Page 98: "School leadership teams that include representatives from all sectors": *Turning Points 2000*, pp. 147–148.

Page 99: "According to *A National Study of Leadership in Middle Level Schools*": Jerry W. Valentine et al., *A National Study of Leadership in Middle Level Schools*, National Association of Secondary School Principals, Reston, Virginia, Vol. 1, 2002, pp. 44–45, 47.

Page 100: "Studies indicate that most parents do not feel qualified": *Playing Their Parts*, New York, Public Agenda, pp. 14–15.

Page 104: "Although research indicates that most people are not involved in their community schools on a regular basis": *Just Waiting to be Asked: A Fresh Look at Attitudes on Public Engagement*, New York, Public Agenda, 2001, pp. 15, 17.

Page 106: "As we are having to do more": Andreae Downs, *Middle Ground*, February 2001, p. 14.

Chapter 8

Page 109: "Get to know me better!": Advice that a 7th grader from Kentucky would give her parents if she could talk to them honestly, data from middle school surveys collected for the book.

Page 110: "Instead of pouting, the Lake Middle cheerleaders": Rhea R. Borja, "Helping Hand," *Education Week*, January 29, 2003, Vol. 22, No. 20, p. 3.

Page 110: "A 2002 survey of students ages 12 through 17 conducted by the nonprofit organization Communities in Schools": "Teens Say Adults Are Critical Support System for Facing Present Fears, Planning Future Success," Nov. 14, 2002 press release, Communities in Schools, www.cisnet.org.

Page 110: "Young people perform important leadership roles:" Domenica Marchetti, "Charity's Youth Movement," *The Chronicle of Philanthropy*, Washington, D.C., January 9, 2003, Vol. XV, No. 6. See also "Youth Involvement: 'No longer a rebellious act'" at www.whatkidscando.org/whatslearned/ youthinvolvement.html.

Page 111: "This generation is just amazing in terms of its desire to give": Domenica Marchetti, *The Chronicle of Philanthropy*.

Page 111: "Just one in 20 adults consistently relates to young people in a positive way": "Grading Grown-Ups 2002: American Adults Report on Their Real Relationships with Kids," Lutheran Brotherhood and Search Institute, www.luthbro.com and www.search-institute.org.

Page 117: "In its 1999 study": *Playing Their Parts: Parents and Teachers Talk About Parental Involvement in Public Schools*, Public Agenda, New York, 1999.

Page 118: "According to an international poll taken in 1998": "The Bottom Line," *NEA Today*, April 1998, p. 8.

Page 122: "I do not assign anything I don't grade and put a comment on": Nancy Paulu, *Helping Your Students with Homework: A Guide for Teachers*, Washington, DC, Office of Educational Research and Improvement, U.S. Department of Education, 1998.

Index

About the Authors

Anthony Jackson is Executive Director, International Studies Secondary Schools Network at the Asia Society. He is co-author or co-editor of two other books on education and inter-ethnic relations among youth, including the landmark study *Turning Points 2000: Educating Adolescents in the 21st Century*. He lives in Southern California with his wife and daughter.

Gayle Andrews, assistant professor at The University of Georgia, served as national director of Carnegie Corporation's Middle Grade School State Policy Initiative and co-wrote, with Anthony Jackson, *Turning Points 2000*. She is a member of National Middle School Association's Research Committee, the National Forum to Accelerate Middle-Grades Reform's Steering Committee, and the Leadership Council for AERA's Middle Level Education Research Special Interest Group. She lives in Athens, Georgia, with her son.

Holly Holland, former editor of National Middle School Association's *Middle Ground* magazine, is the author or co-author of three other books about education and serves on the board of the Kentucky Advisory Council for Gifted and Talented Education. She lives in Louisville, Kentucky, with her husband (a middle school teacher) and two children.

Priscilla Pardini, a former middle-grades language arts teacher and education reporter for the *Milwaukee Journal*, is currently a freelance writer and editor specializing in education. She lives in Shorewood, Wisconsin, with her husband and son.